The Joy of Irish F[olk Songs]

Edited and arranged by Jack Long

This publication is not authorised for sale in
the United States of America and/or Canada.

Yorktown Music Press / Music Sales Limited
London / New York / Paris / Sydney / Copenhagen / Madrid

Exclusive Distributors:
Music Sales Limited
8/9 Frith Street, London W1V 5TZ, England.
Music Sales Pty Limited
120 Rothschild Avenue, Rosebery, NSW 2018, Australia.

This book © Copyright 1997 by Yorktown Music Press/Music Sales Limited.
Order No. YK20626
ISBN 0-7119-6463-7

Cover illustration by Anthony Sidwell.
Compiled by Peter Evans.
Music edited and arranged by Jack Long.
Music processed by Enigma Music Production Services.

Music Sales' complete catalogue describes thousands of titles and
is available in full colour sections by subject, direct from Music Sales Limited.
Please state your areas of interest and send a cheque/postal order for £1.50 for postage to:
Music Sales Limited, Newmarket Road, Bury St. Edmunds, Suffolk IP33 3YB.

Visit the Internet Music Shop at http://www.musicsales.co.uk

Your Guarantee of Quality:
As publishers, we strive to produce every book to the highest commercial standards.
The music has been freshly engraved and the book has been carefully designed to minimise awkward page turns and to make playing from it a real pleasure.
Particular care has been given to specifying acid-free, neutral-sized paper made from pulps which have not been elemental chlorine bleached.
This pulp is from farmed sustainable forests and was produced with special regard for the environment.
Throughout, the printing and binding have been planned to ensure a sturdy, attractive publication which should give years of enjoyment.
If your copy fails to meet our high standards, please inform us and we will gladly replace it.

Unauthorised reproduction of any part of this publication by
any means including photocopying is an infringement of copyright.

Printed in the United Kingdom by
Caligraving Limited, Thetford, Norfolk.

The Black Velvet Band 6
A Bunch Of Thyme 4
Cockles And Mussels 12
Come Back To Erin 9
Dear Old Donegal 14
Galway Bay 18
The Harp That Once Thro' Tara's Halls 21
If You're Irish Come Into The Parlour 22
The Isle Of Innisfree 26
It's A Long Way To Tipperary 29
The Minstrel Boy 32
The Mountains Of Mourne 50
My Wild Irish Rose 34
The Old Rustic Bridge By The Mill 38
Paddy McGinty's Goat 42
Phil The Fluter 45
Rose Of Tralee 48
The Spinning Wheel 53
Too-Ra-Loo-Ra-Loo-Ral (That's An Irish Lullaby) 56
When Irish Eyes Are Smiling 58
Whistling Gypsy (The Gypsy Rover) 62

A Bunch Of Thyme

Traditional Irish Song

3. Once she had a bunch of thyme;
   She thought it never would decay.
   Then came a lusty sailor
   Who chanced to pass her way:
   He stole her bunch of thyme away.

4. The sailor gave to her a rose,
   A rose that never would decay.
   He gave it to her
   To keep her reminded
   Of when he stole her thyme away.

5. For thyme it is a precious thing.
   And thyme brings all things to my mind.
   Thyme with all its labours,
   Along with all its joys,
   Thyme brings all things to an end.

The Black Velvet Band

Irish Traditional

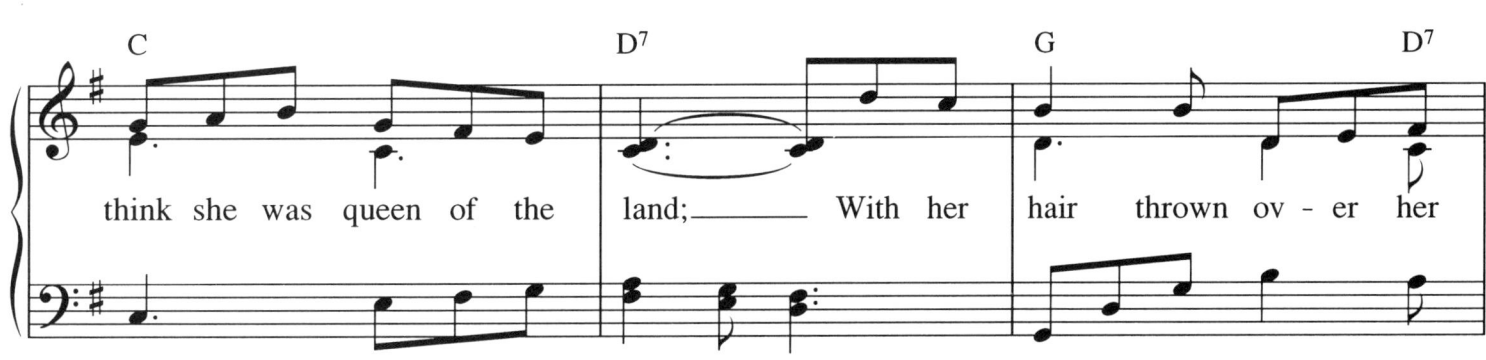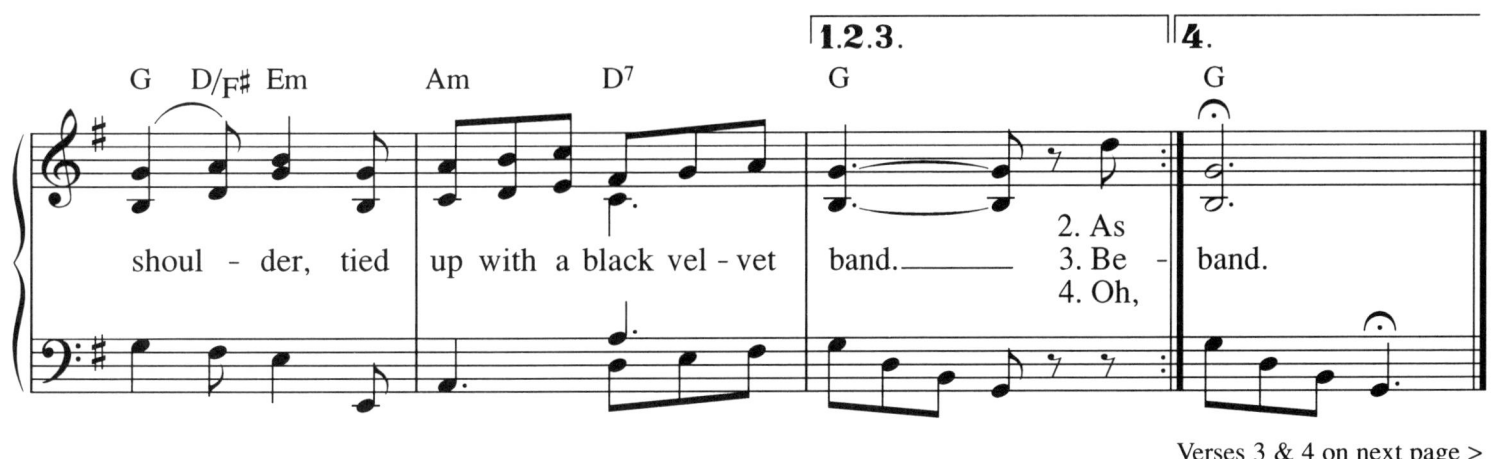

3. Before the judge and the jury the both of us had to appear,
   And a gentleman swore to the jewel'ry; the case against us was clear.
   For seven years transportation right unto Van Dieman's Land,
   Far away from my friends and relations, to follow her black velvet band.
   Her eyes they shone like diamonds (etc.)

4. Oh, all you brave young Irish lads, a warning take by me:
   Beware of the pretty young damsels that are knocking around in Tralee!
   They'll treat you to whiskey and porter until you're unable to stand,
   And before you have time for to leave them you are unto Van Dieman's Land.
   Her eyes they shone like diamonds (etc.)

Come Back To Erin

Irish Traditional

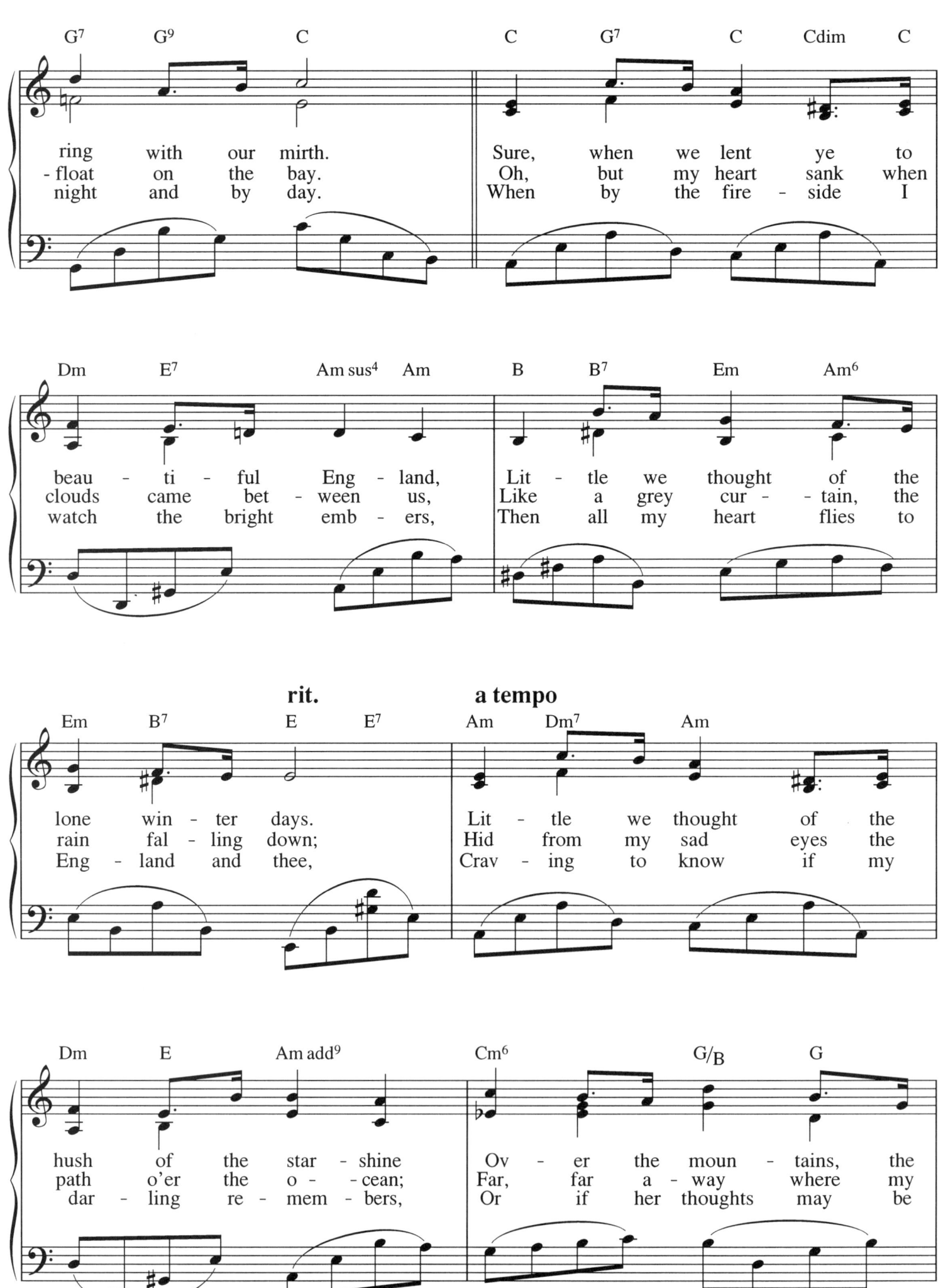

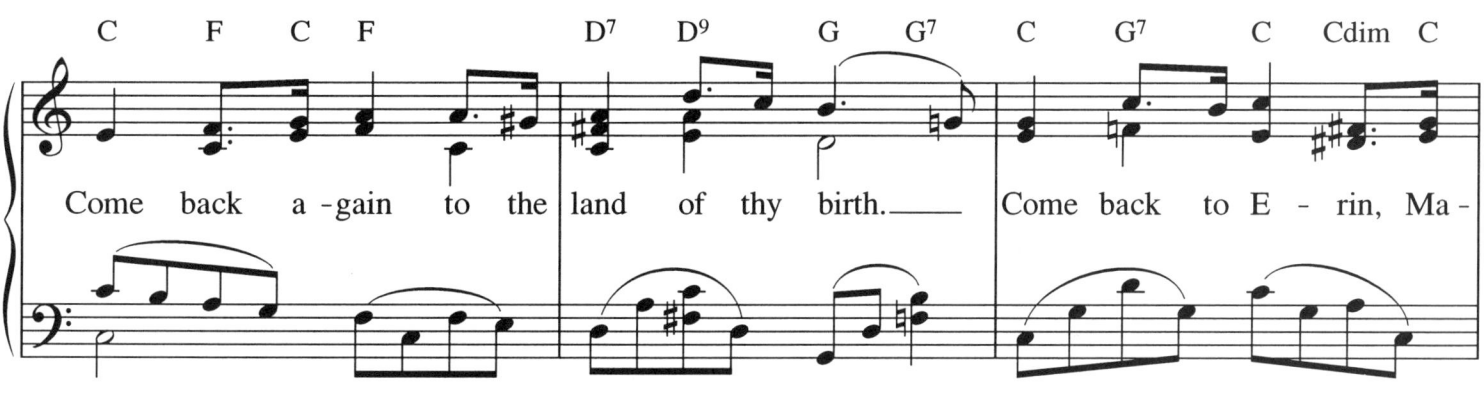

Cockles And Mussels

Traditional

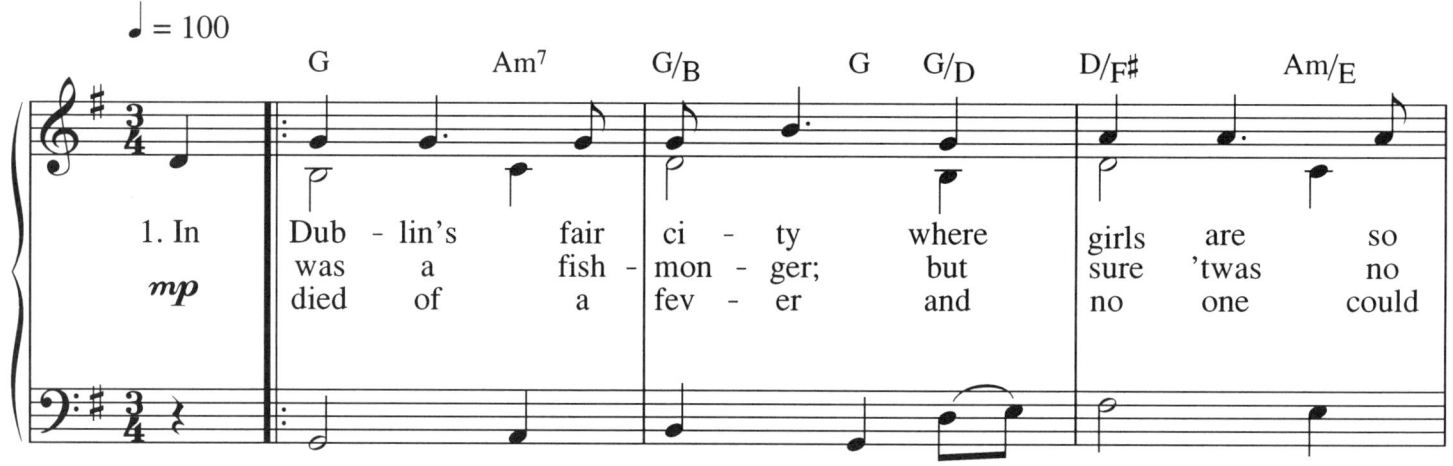

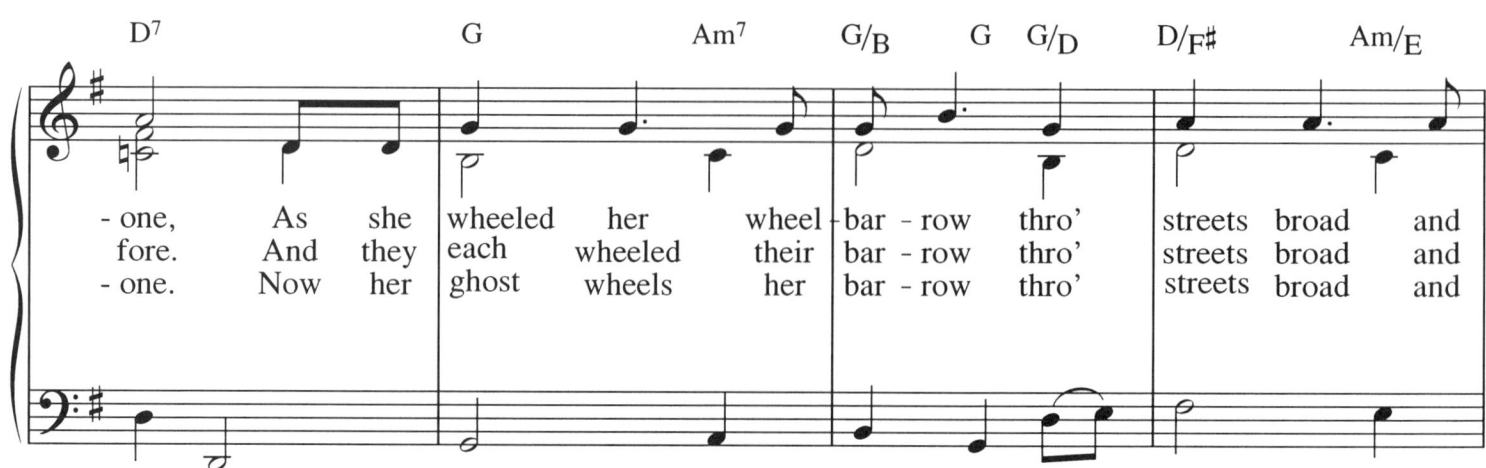

© Copyright 1997 Dorsey Brothers Music Limited, 8/9 Frith Street, London W1.
All Rights Reserved. International Copyright Secured.

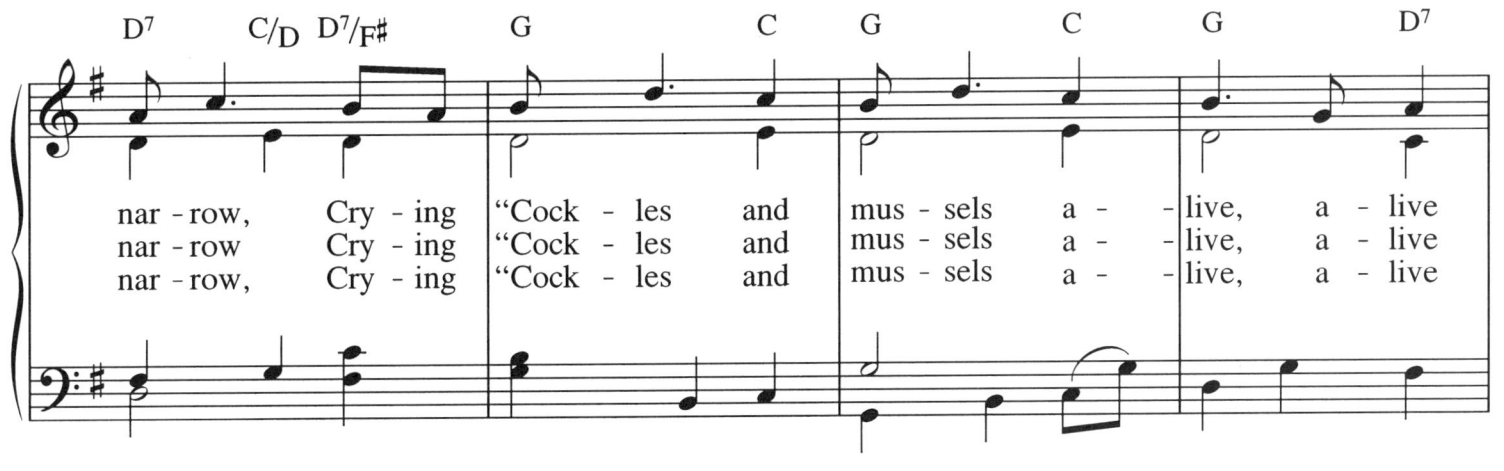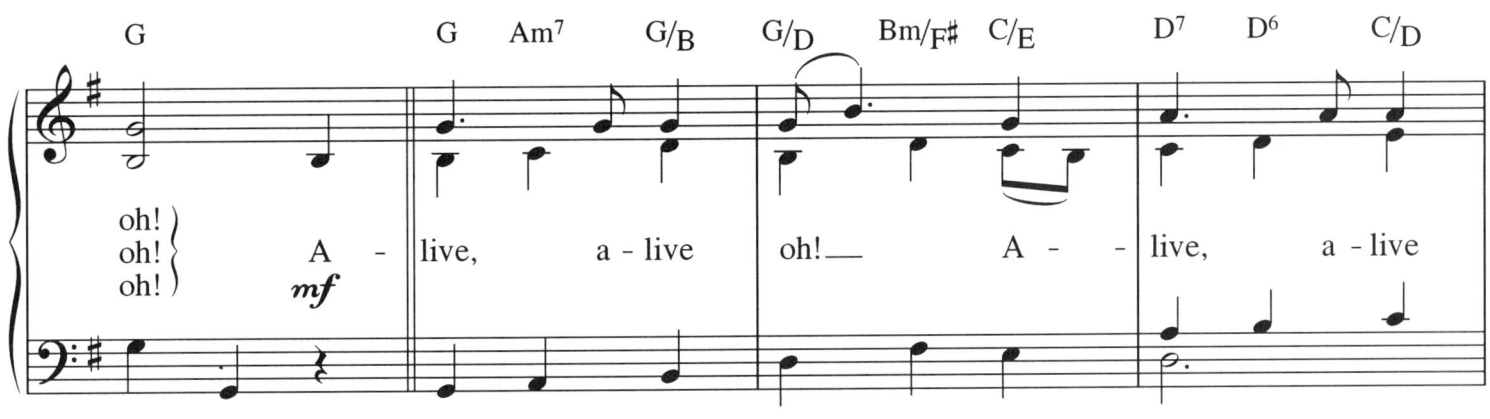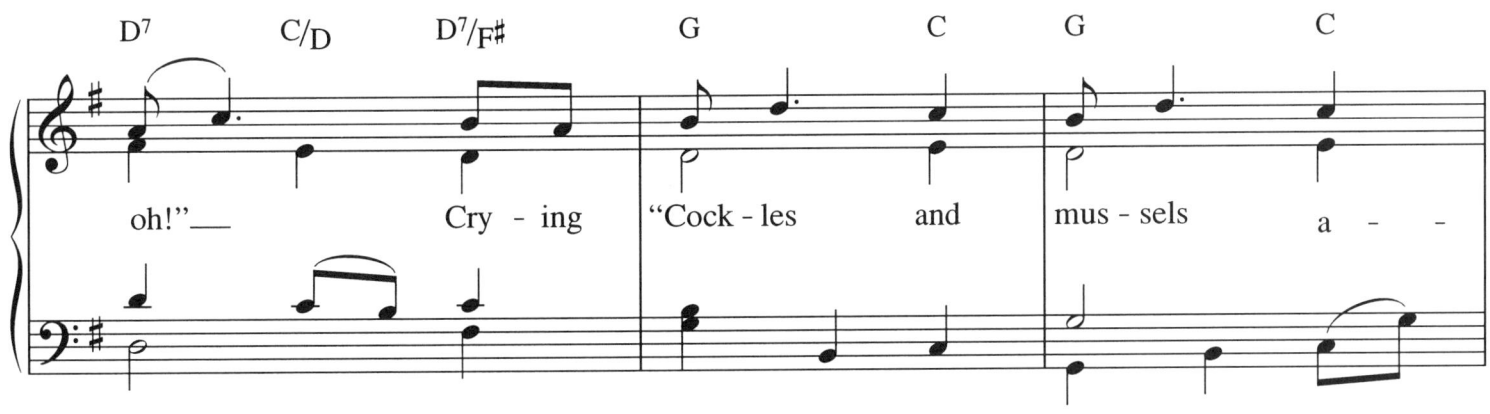

Dear Old Donegal

Words & Music by Steve Graham

Galway Bay

Words & Music by Dr Arthur Colahan

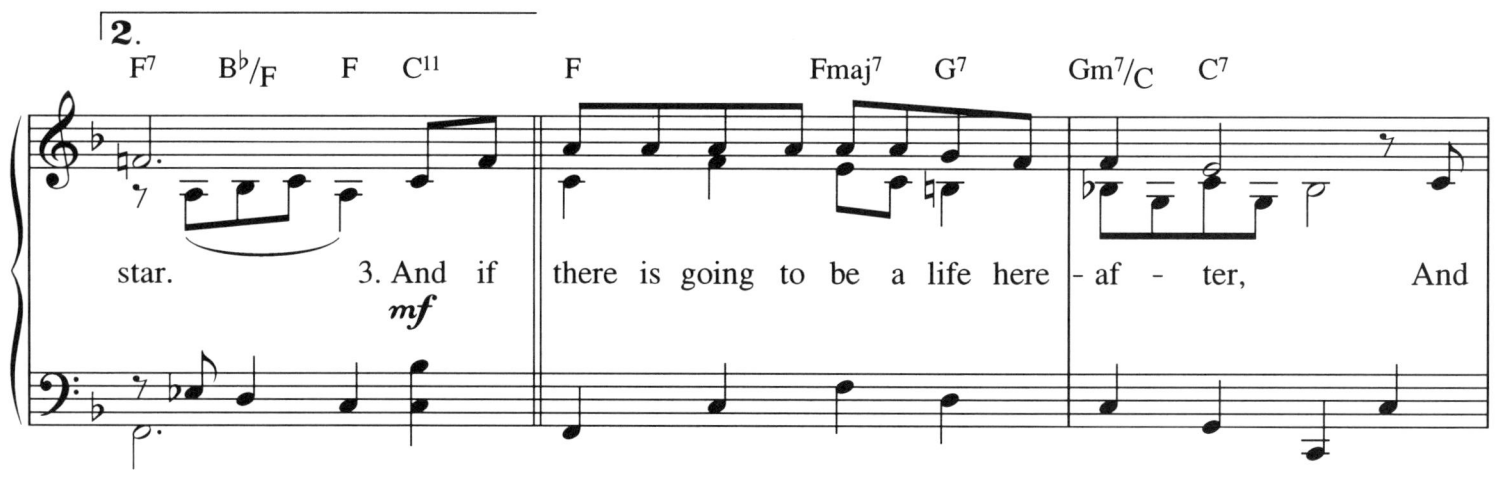
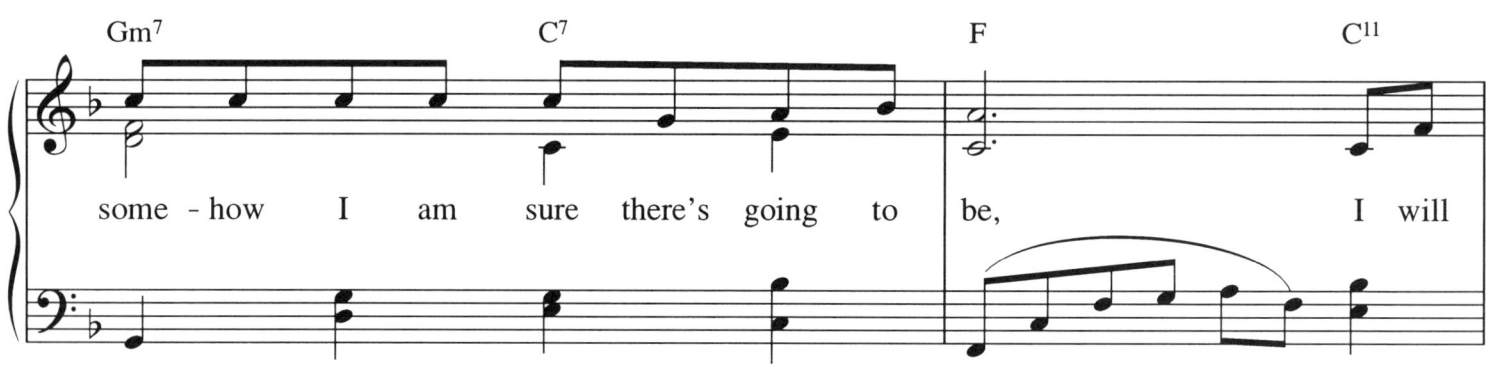

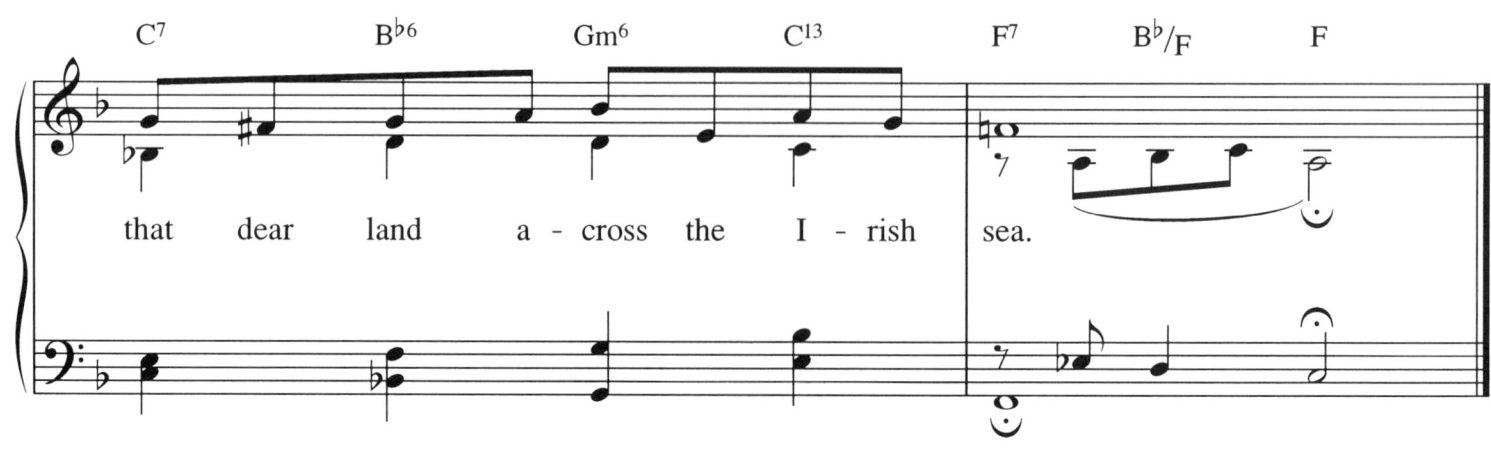

The Harp That Once Thro' Tara's Halls

Words & Music by Thomas Moore

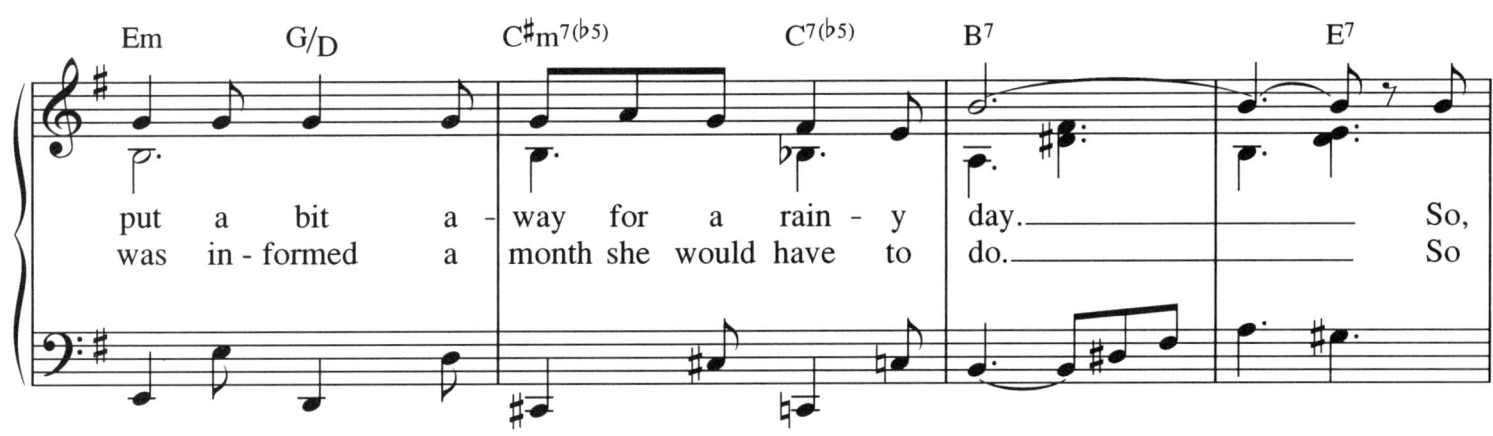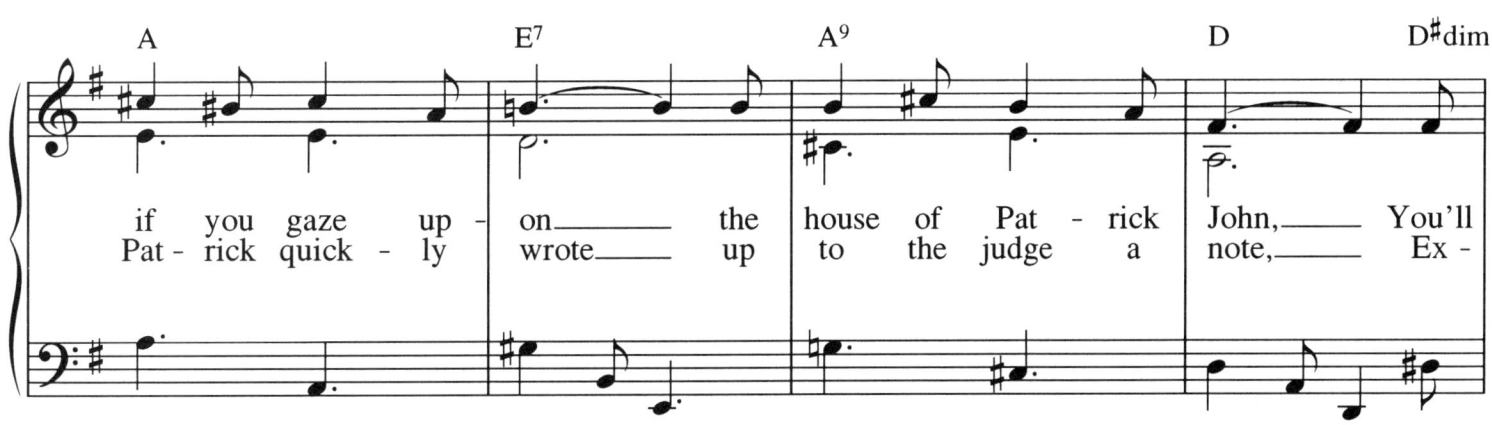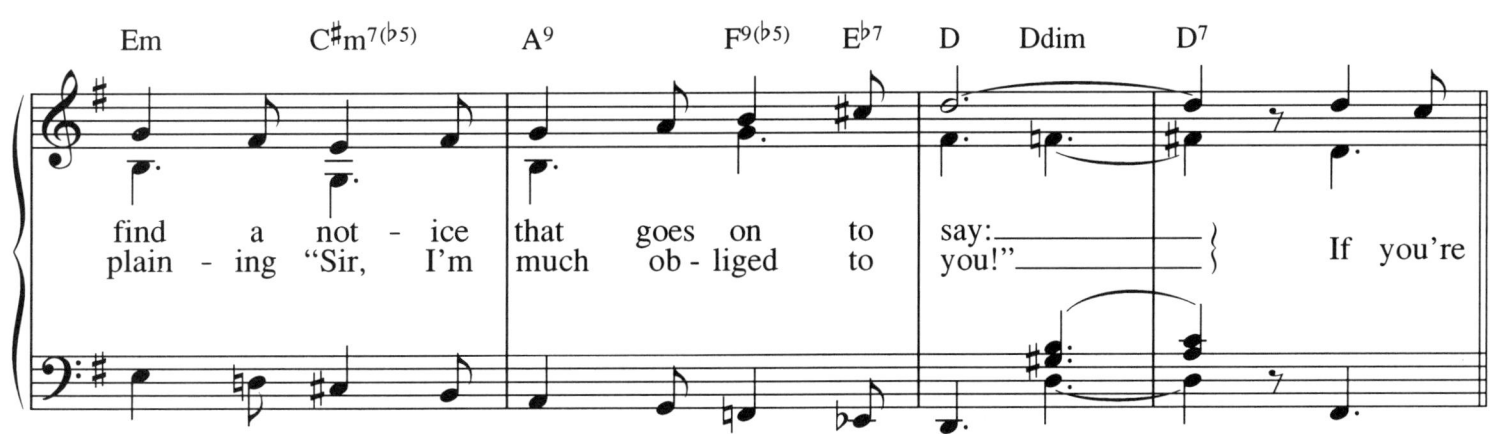

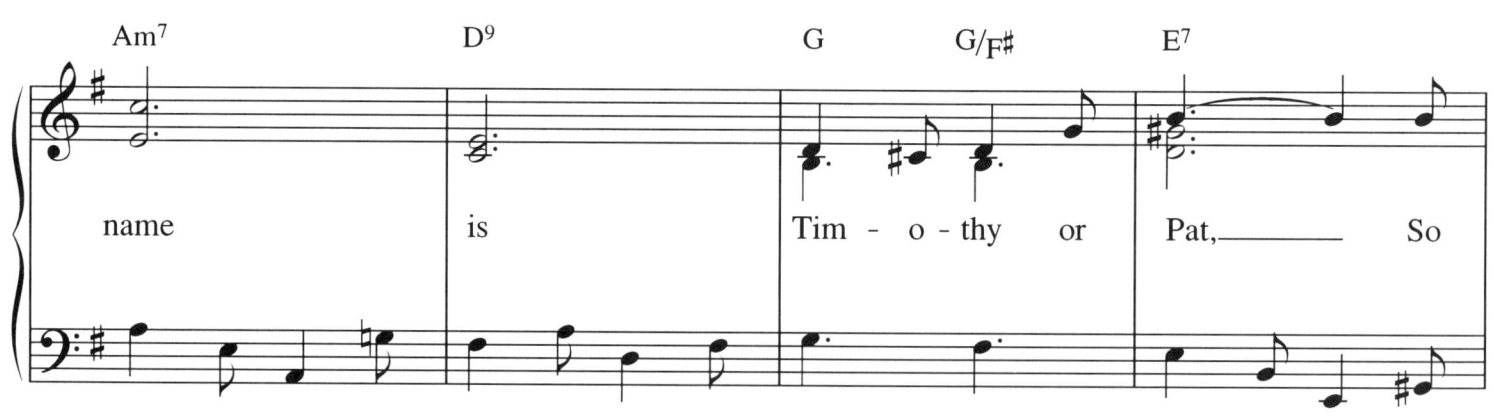

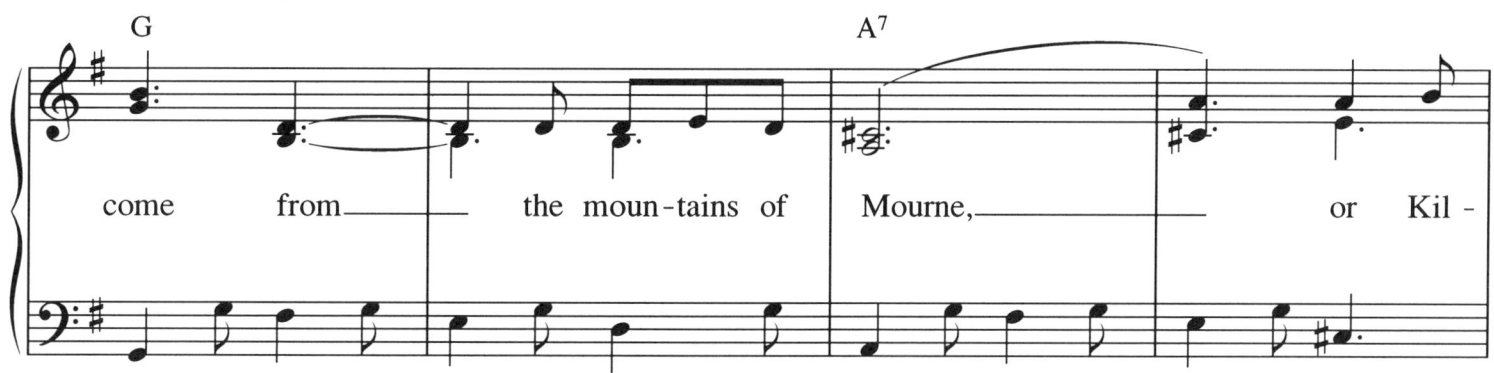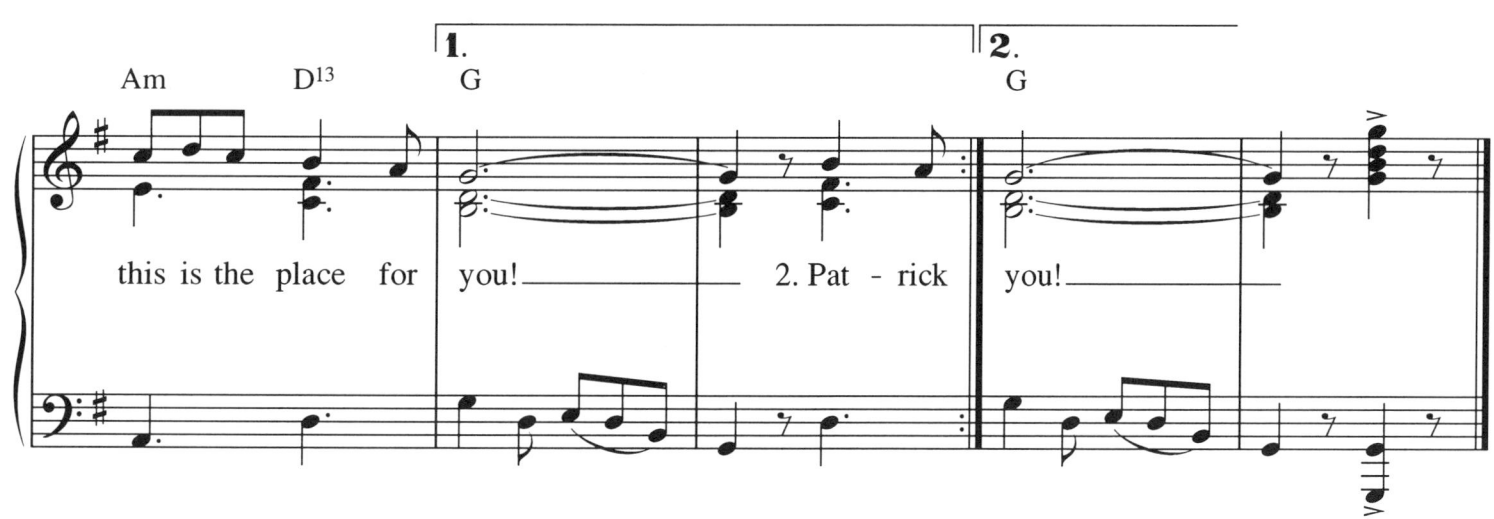

The Isle Of Innisfree

Words & Music by Dick Farrelly

© Copyright 1950 Reproduced by permission of Peter Maurice Music Company Limited, 127 Charing Cross Road, London WC2.
All Rights Reserved. International Copyright Secured.

It's A Long Way To Tipperary

Words & Music by Jack Judge & Harry Williams

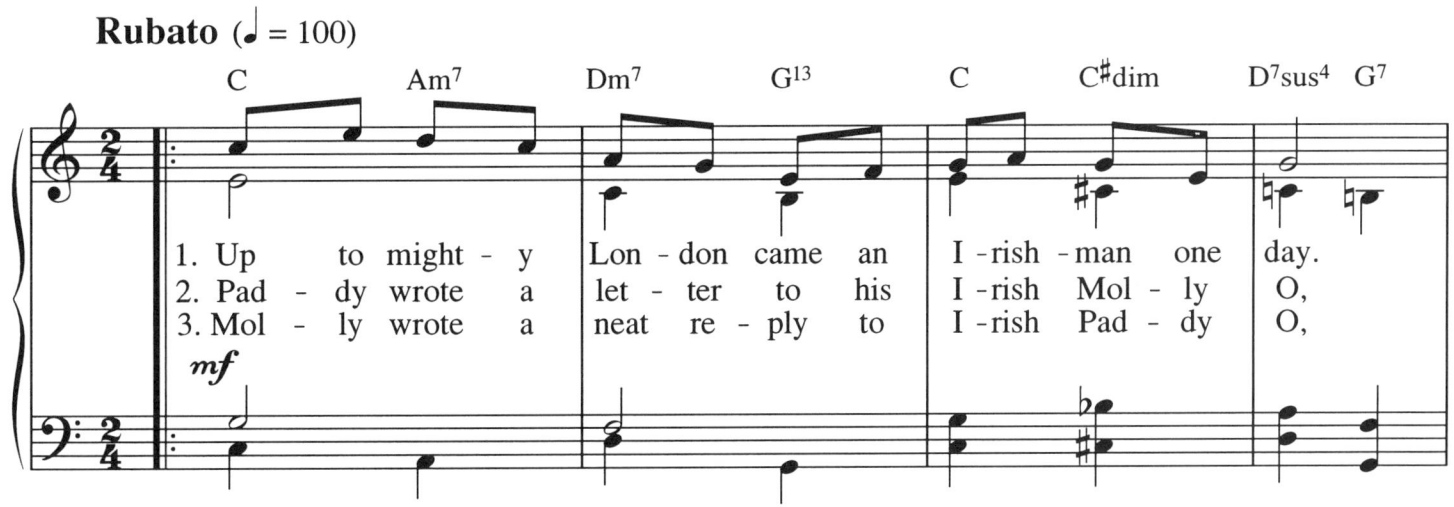

1. Up to mighty London came an Irishman one day.
2. Paddy wrote a letter to his Irish Molly O,
3. Molly wrote a neat reply to Irish Paddy O,

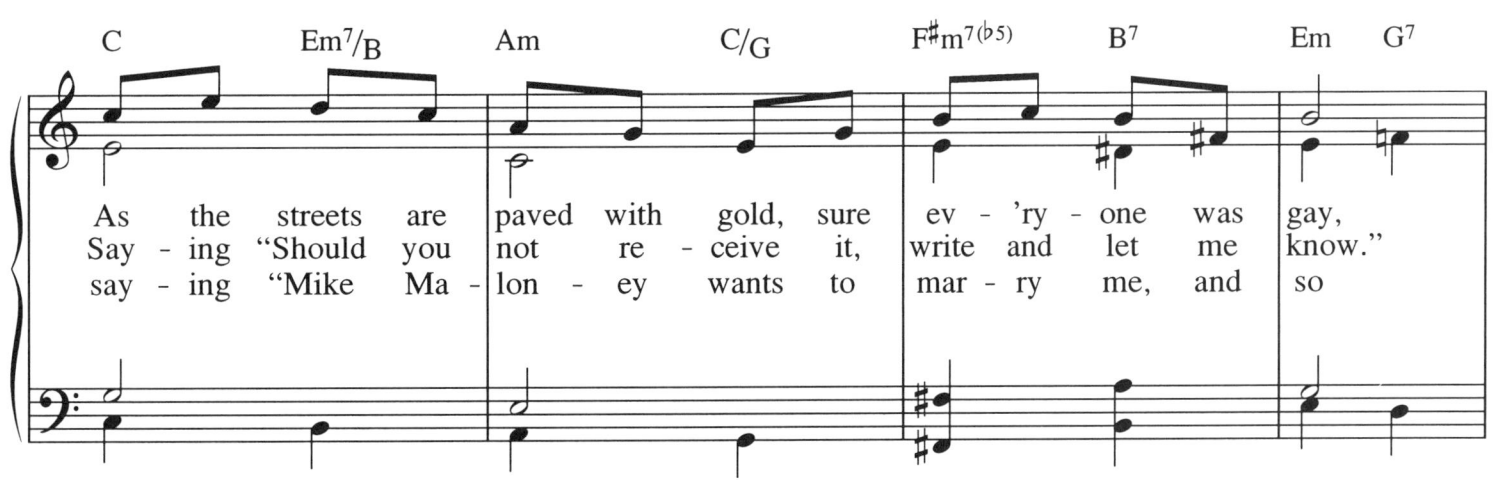

As the streets are paved with gold, sure ev'ryone was gay,
Saying "Should you not receive it, write and let me know."
saying "Mike Maloney wants to marry me, and so

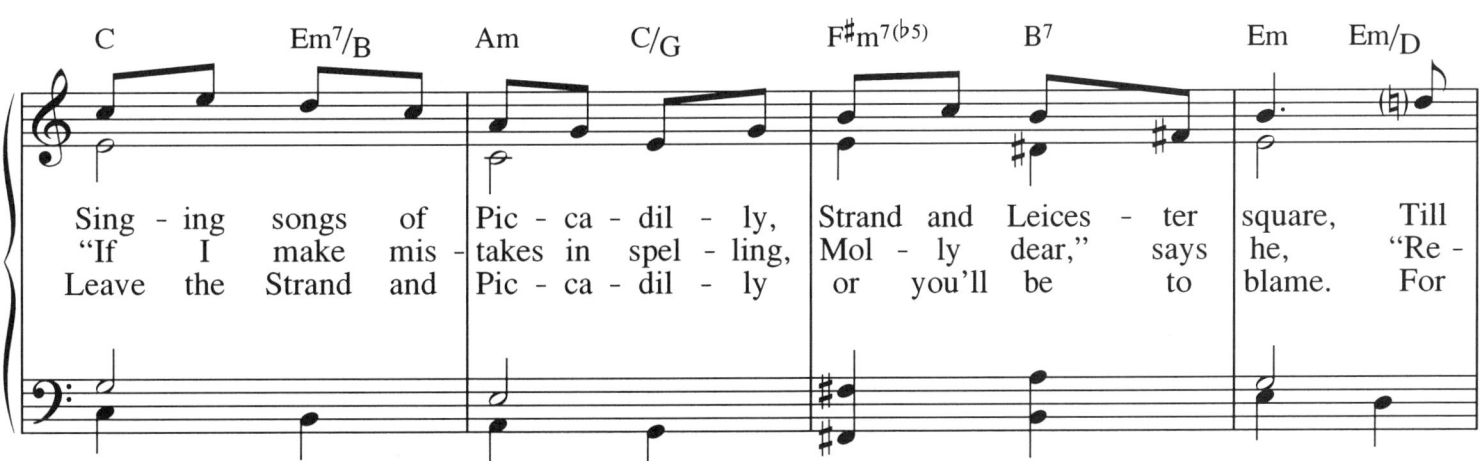

Singing songs of Piccadilly, Strand and Leicester square, Till
"If I make mistakes in spelling, Molly dear," says he, "Re-
Leave the Strand and Piccadilly or you'll be to blame. For

© Copyright 1997 Dorsey Brothers Music Limited, 8/9 Frith Street, London W1.
All Rights Reserved. International Copyright Secured.

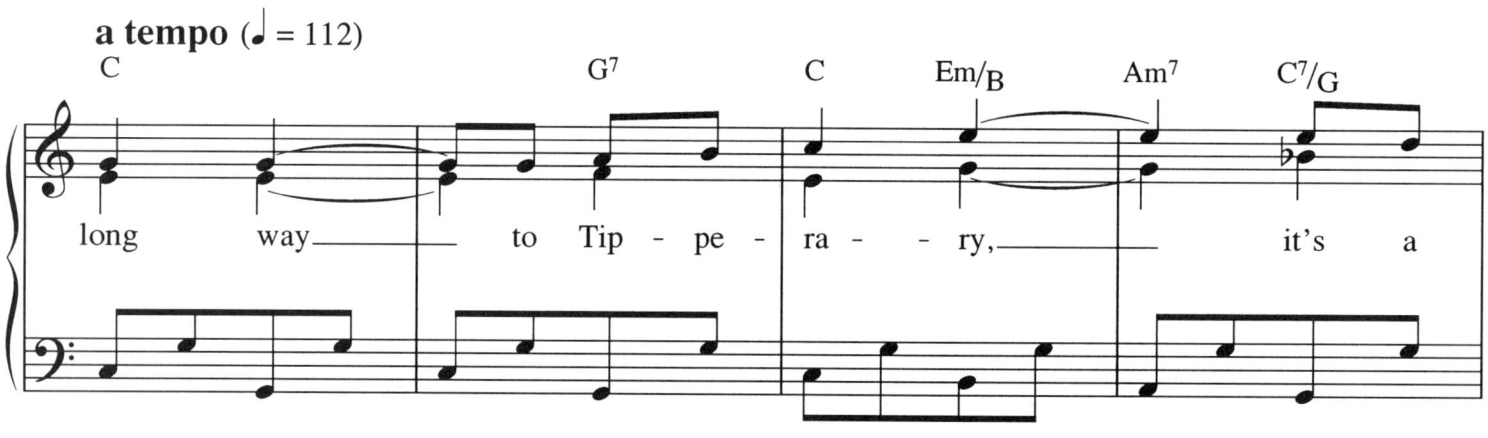
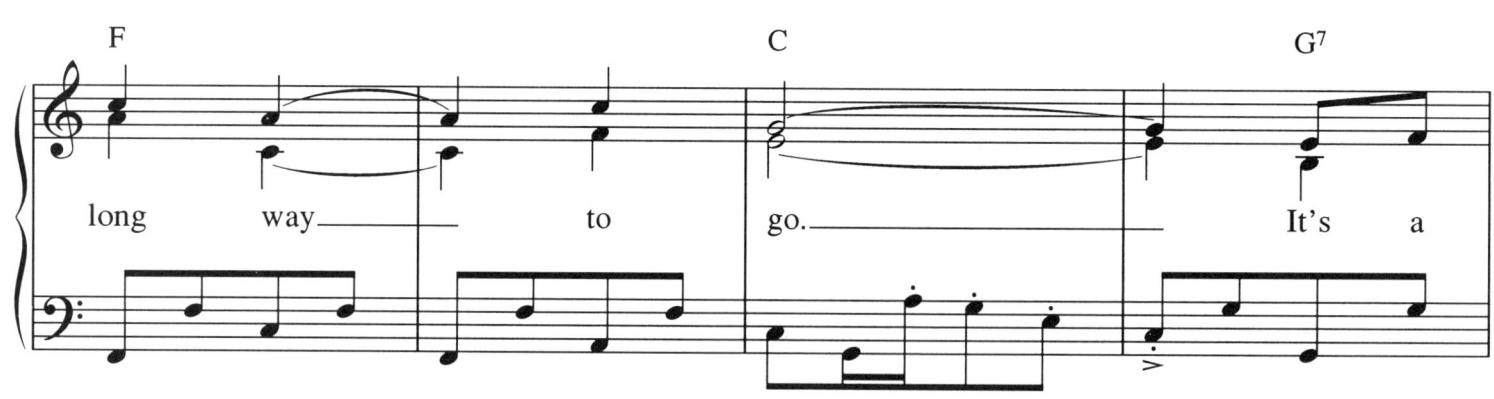
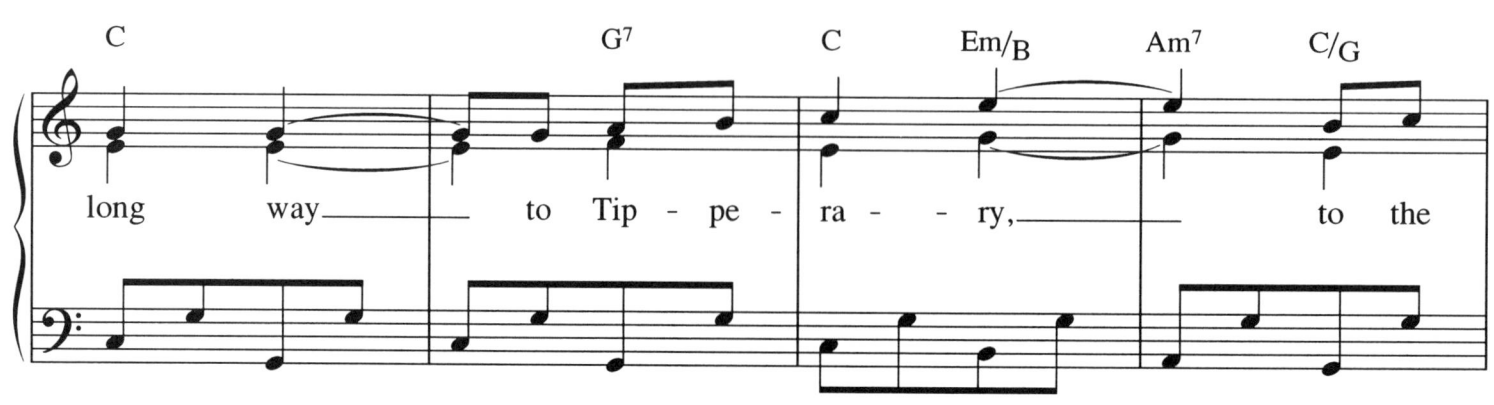

The Minstrel Boy

Traditional

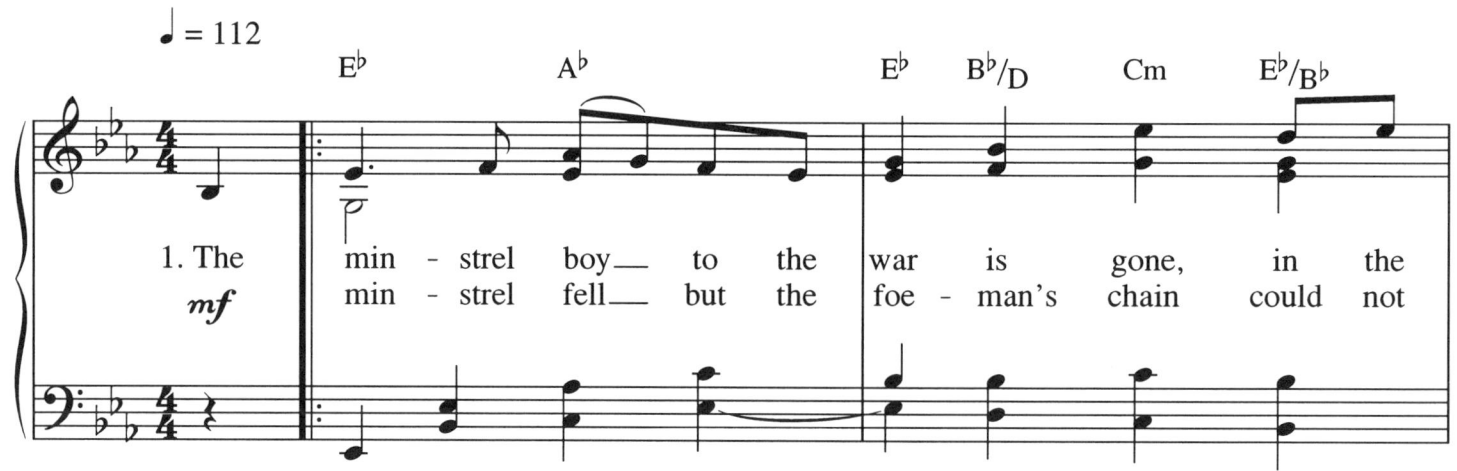

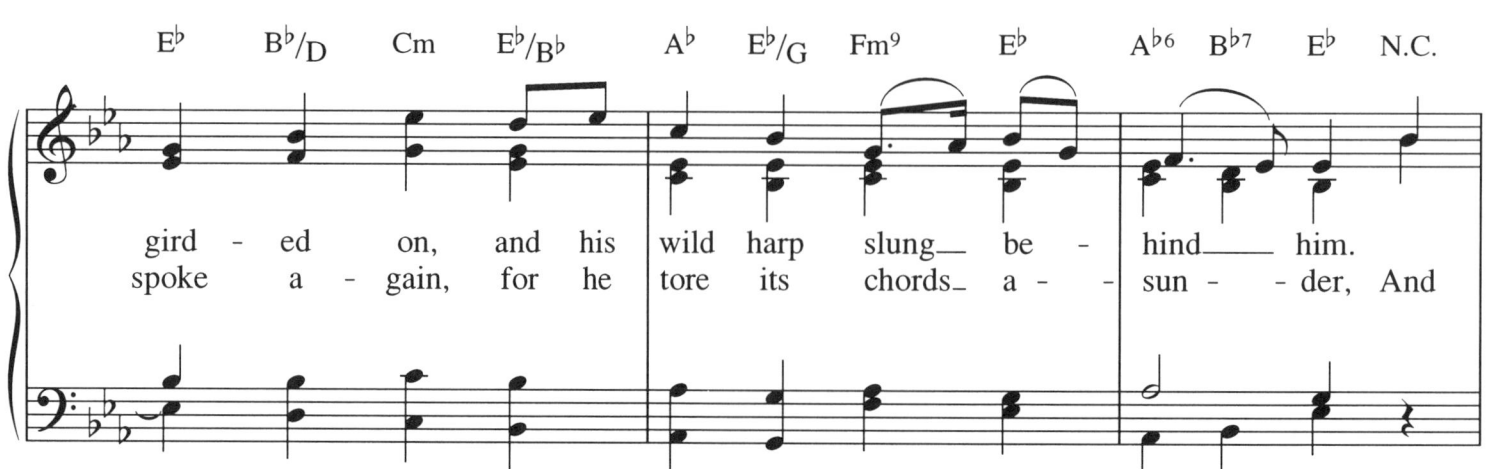

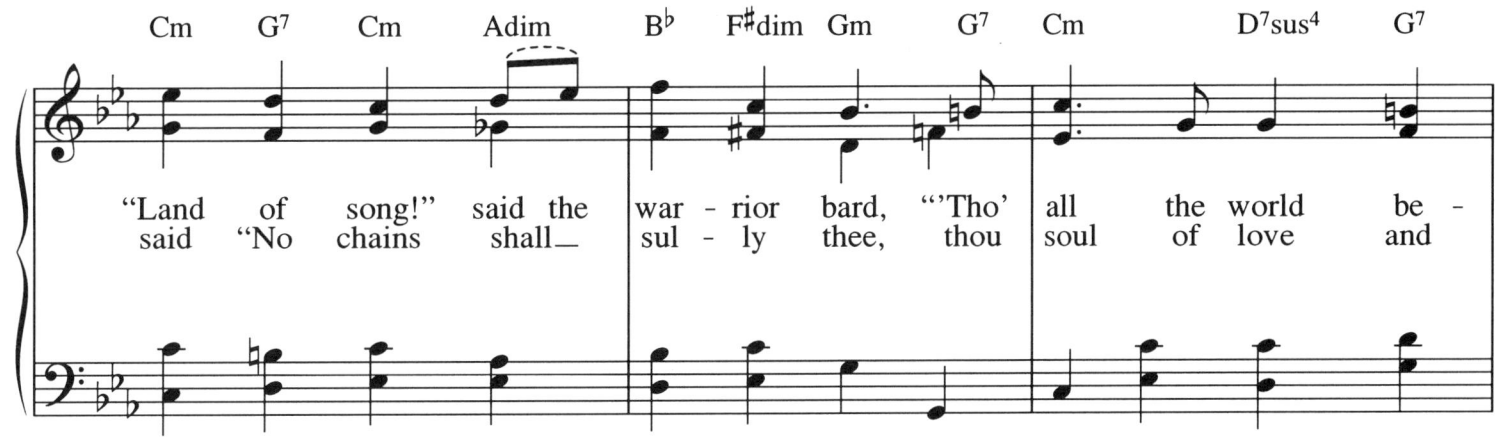
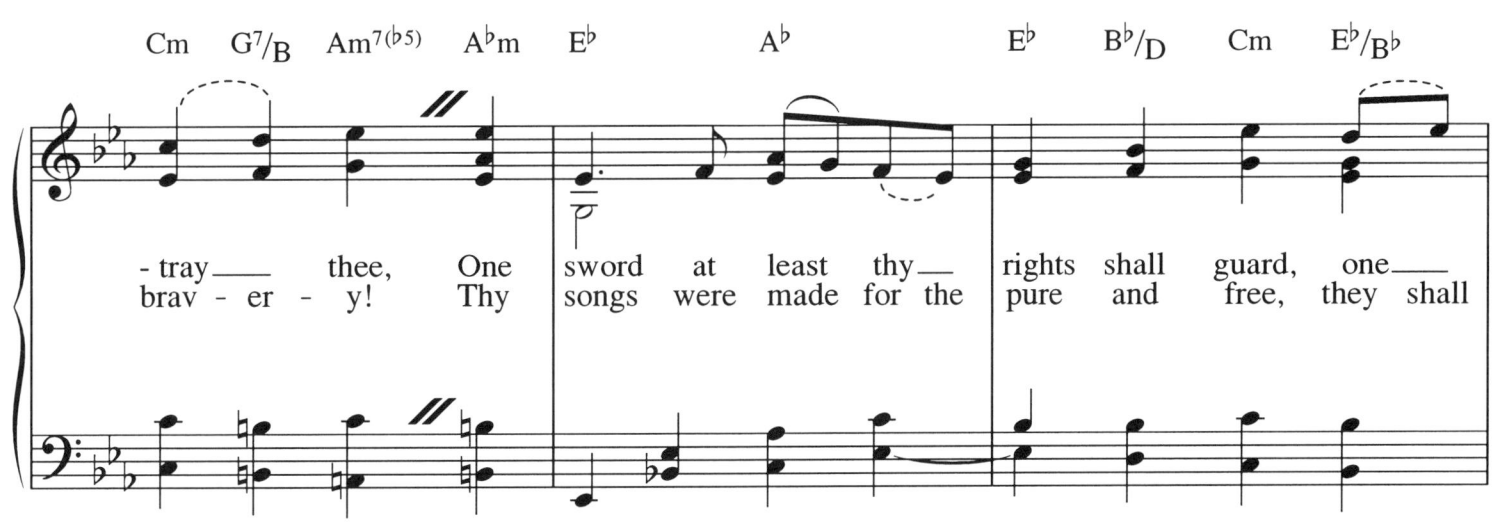
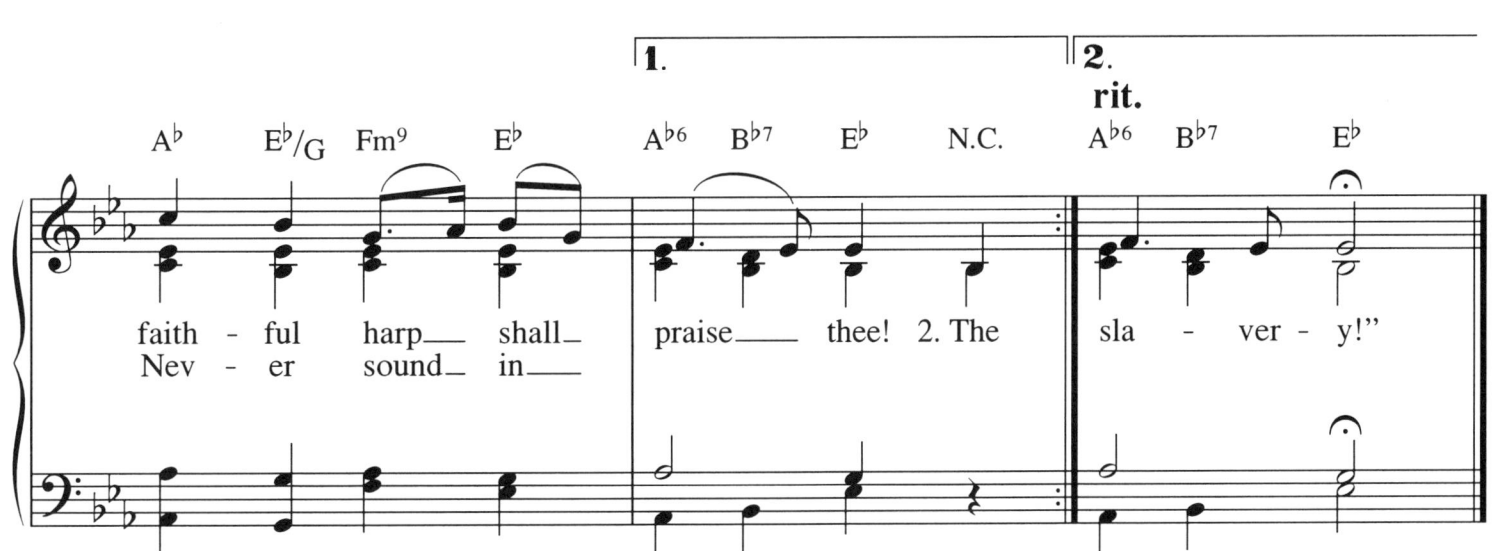

My Wild Irish Rose

Words & Music by Chauncey Olcott

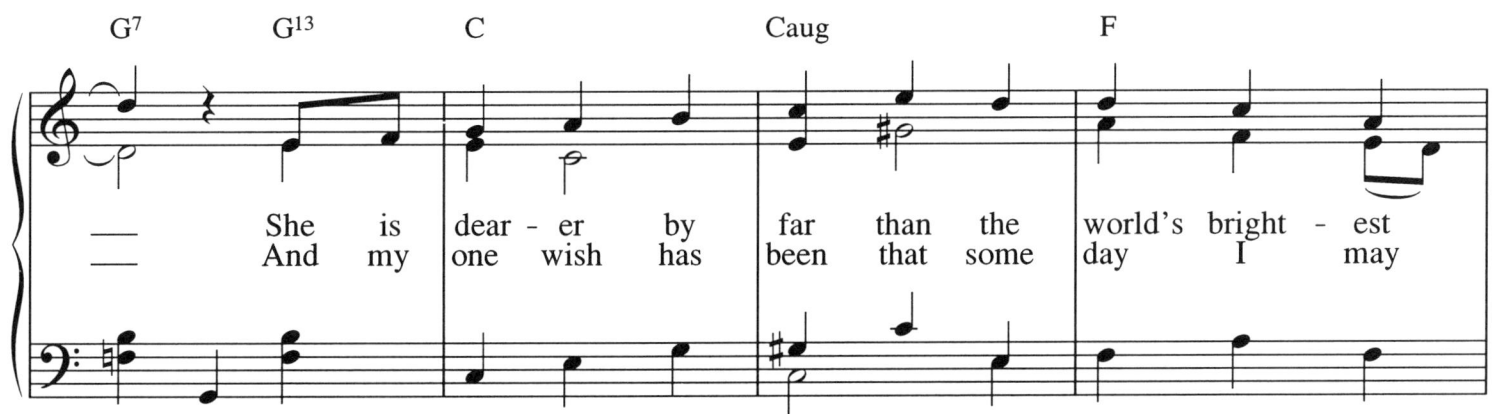

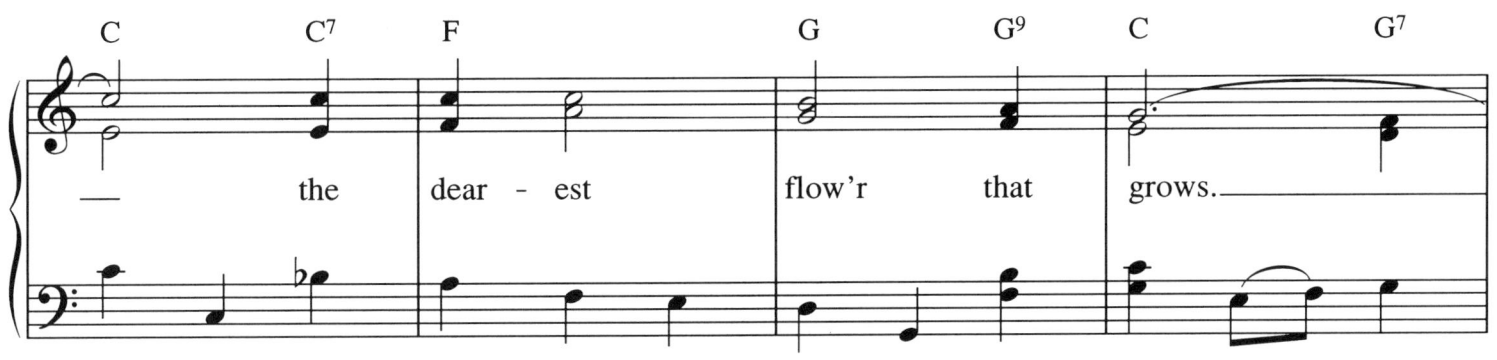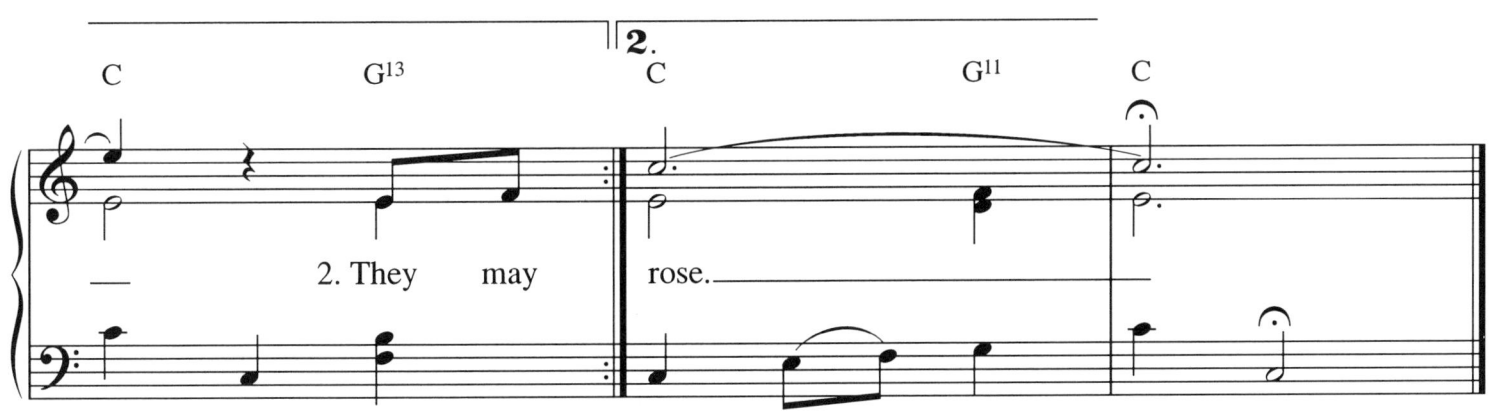

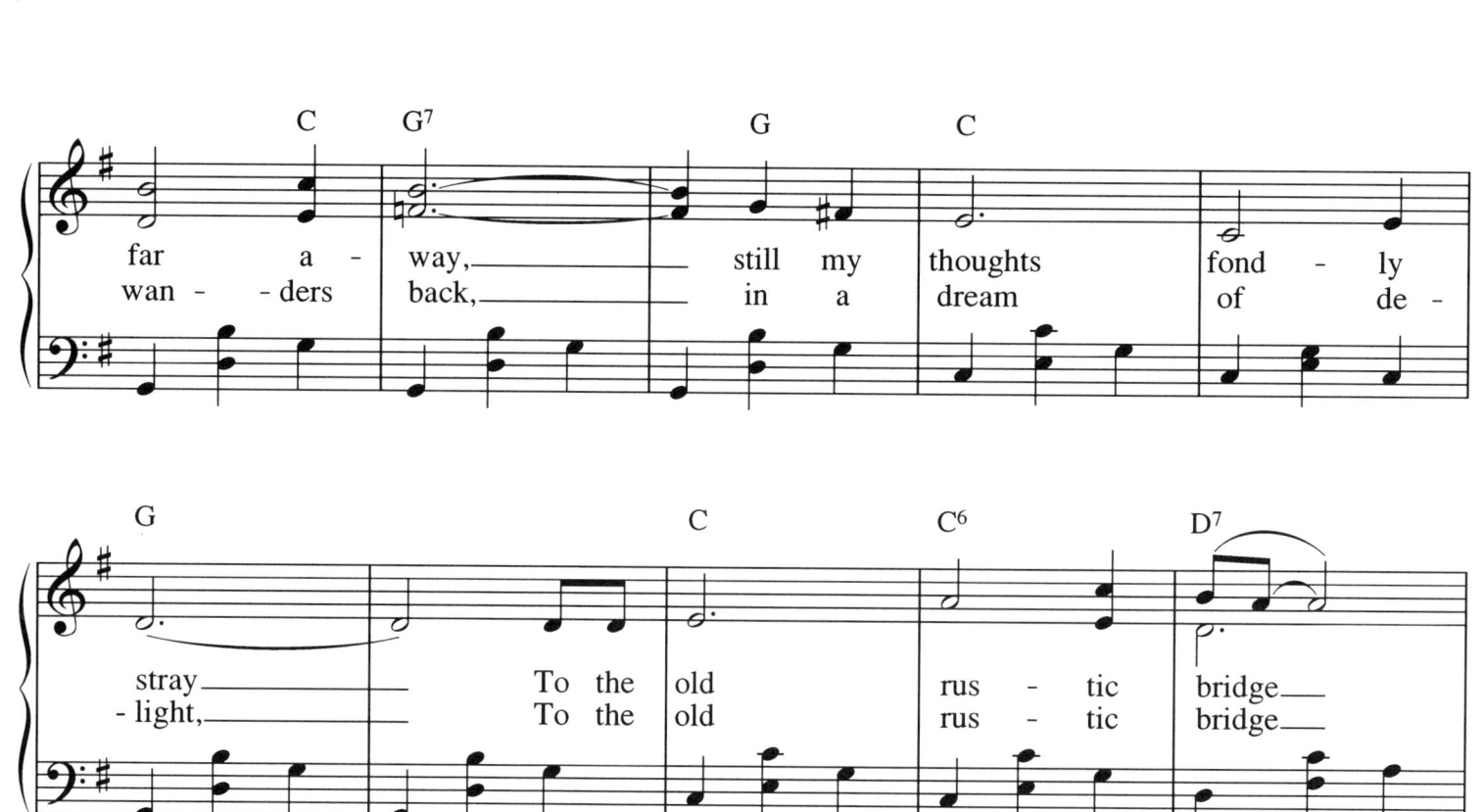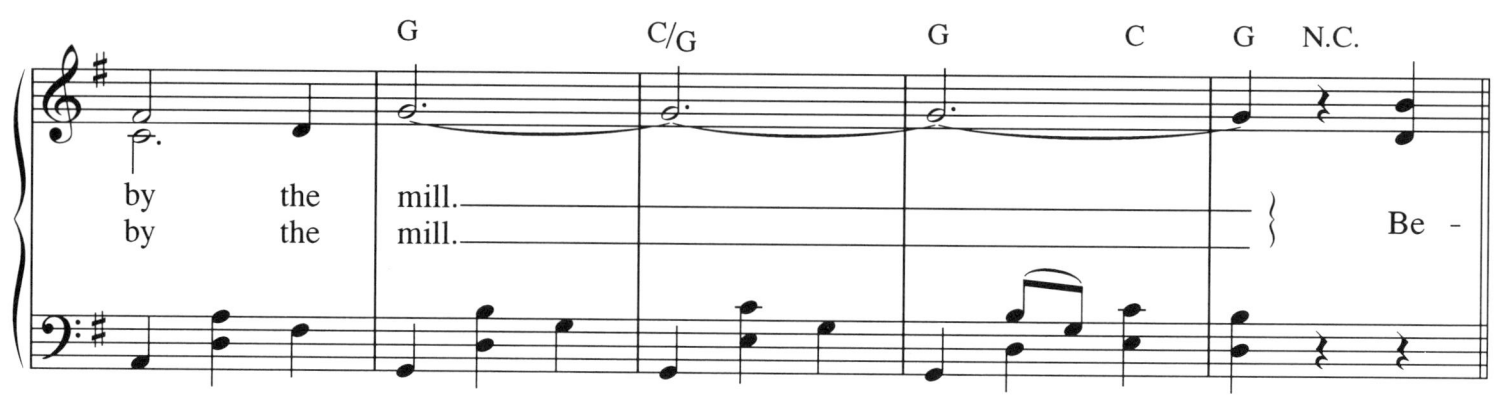

Paddy McGinty's Goat

Words & Music by Bert Lee & R. P. Weston

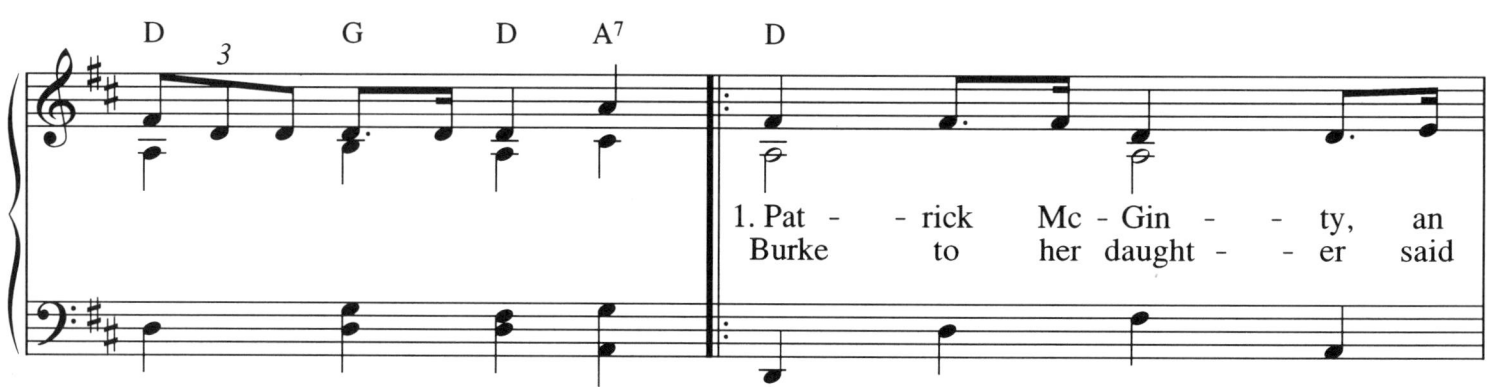

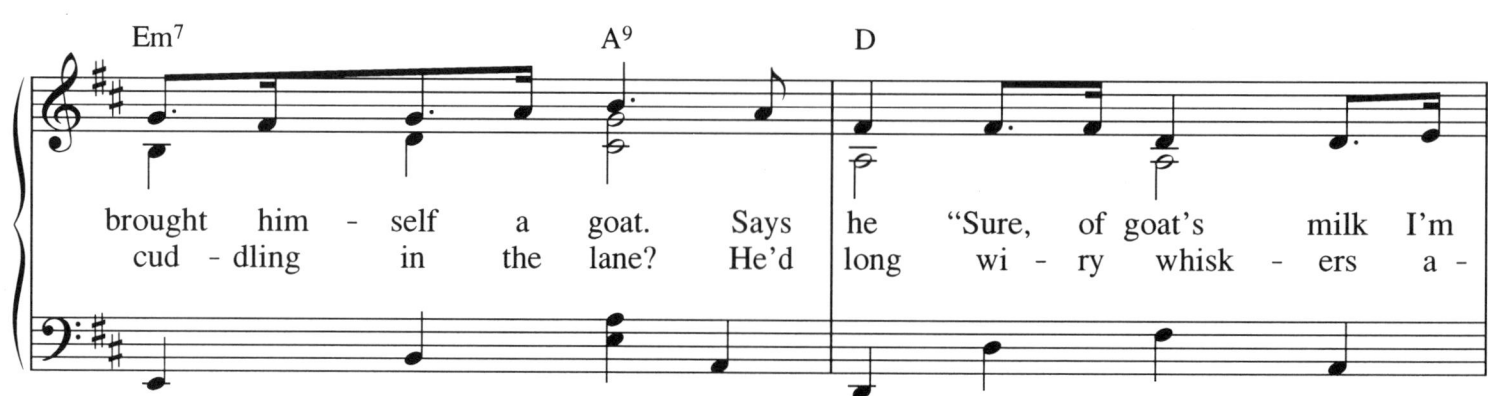

1. Pat-rick Mc-Gin-ty, an I-rish man of note, Fell in for a for-tune and he brought him-self a goat. Says he "Sure, of goat's milk I'm

Burke to her daught-er said "Lis-ten Ma-ry Jane, Who was the man you were cud-dling in the lane? He'd long wi-ry whisk-ers a-

© Copyright 1917 Reproduced by permission of Francis Day & Hunter Limited, 127 Charing Cross Road, London WC2.
All Rights Reserved. International Copyright Secured.

3. Now Norah McCarthy the knot was goin' to tie;
   She washed out her trousseau and hung it out to dry.
   Along came the goat and he saw the bits of white,
   And chewed up all her falderals upon the wedding night!
   "Oh, turn out the light quick," she shouted out to Pat,
   "For tho' I'm your bride, sure I'm not worth looking at.
   I had two of everything, I told you when I wrote,
   But now I've one of nothing all through Paddy McGinty's goat!"

4. Mickey Riley, he went to the races t'other day.
   He won twenty pounds and shouted "Hip-hoo-ray!"
   He held up the note, shouting "Look at what I've got!"
   The goat came up and grabbed at it and swallowed up the lot!
   "He's eaten me bank note," says Mickey, with the hump.
   They went for the doctor and they got a stomach pump.
   They pumped and they pumped for the twenty pound note,
   But all they got was ninepence out of Paddy McGinty's goat!

5. Now ould Paddy's goat had a wondrous appetite,
   And one day for breakfast he had some dynamite;
   A big box of matches he swallowed all serene,
   Then out he went and swallowed up a quart of 'parafeen'.
   He sat by the fireside, he did'nt give a hang,
   He swallowed a spark and exploded with a bang!
   So if you go to heaven, you can bet a dollar note
   The angel with the whiskers on is Paddy McGinty's goat!

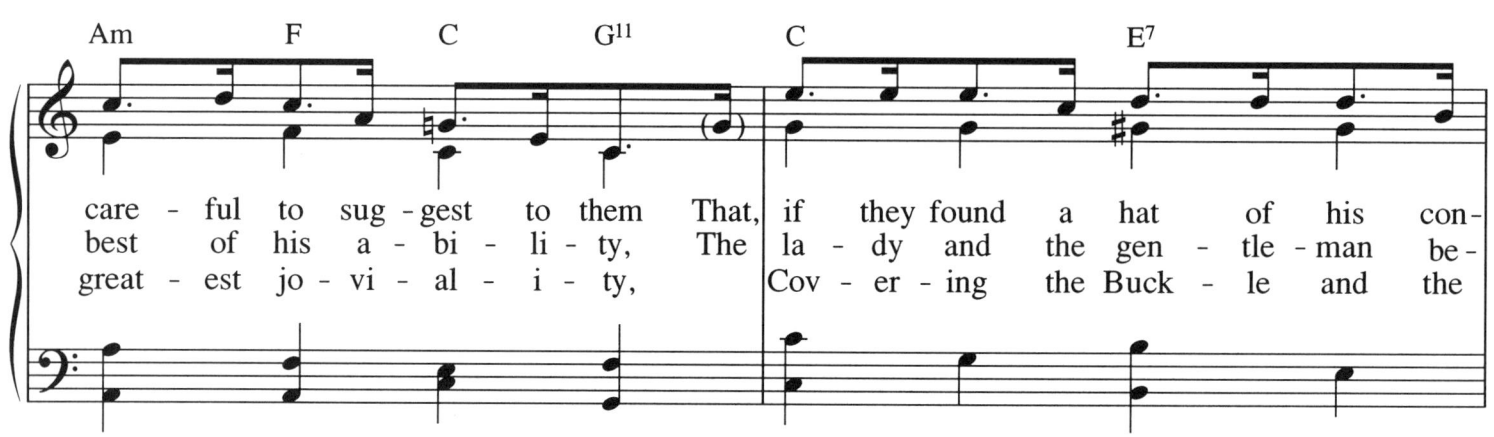
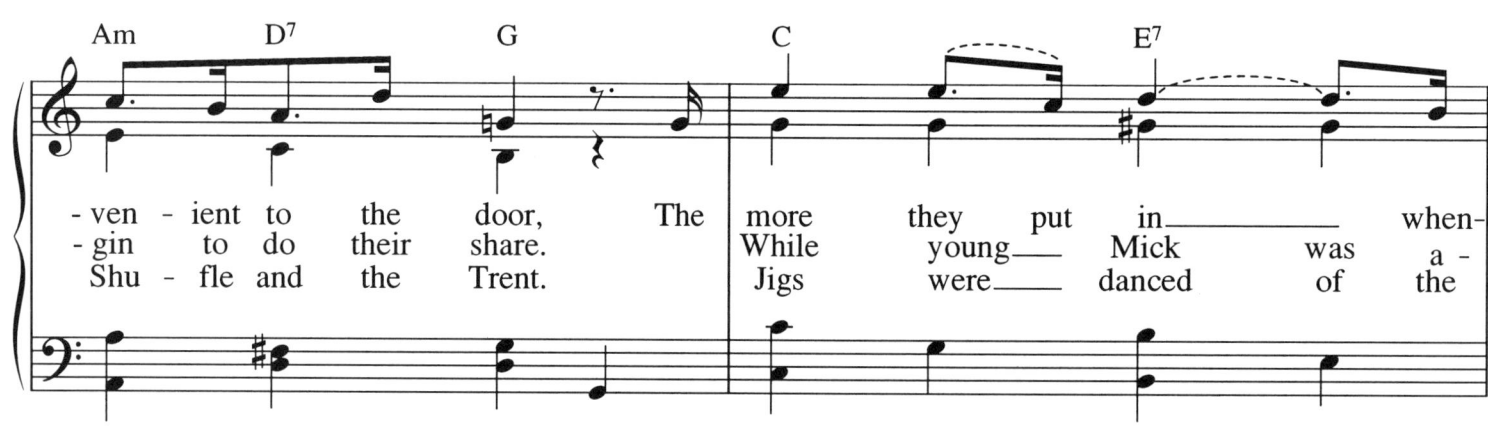
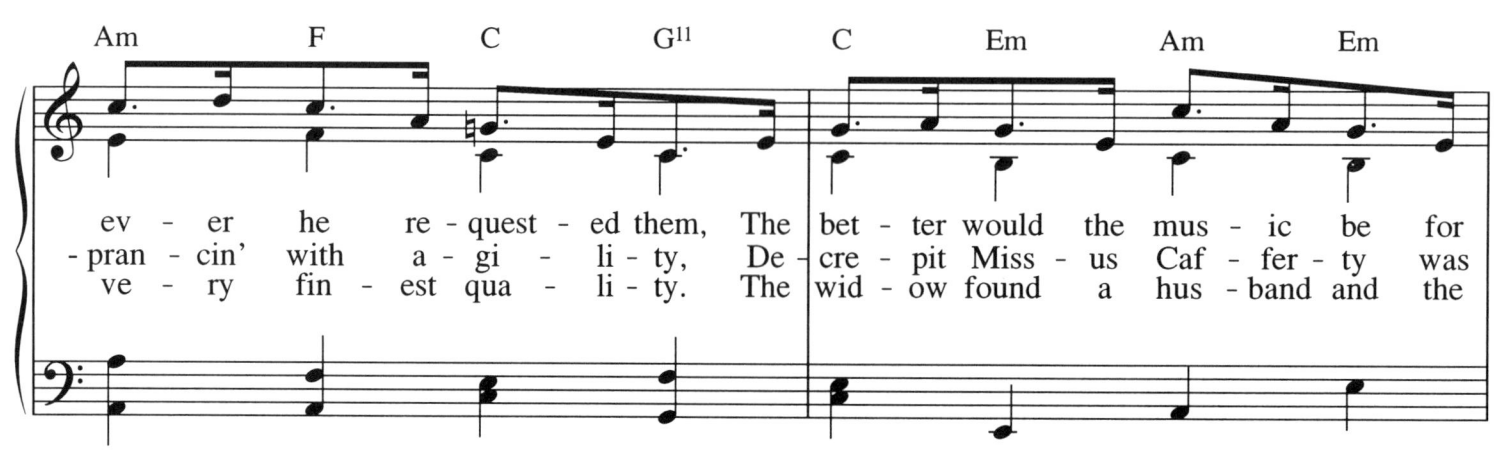

The Mountains Of Mourne

Words & Music by Percy French & Houston Collisson

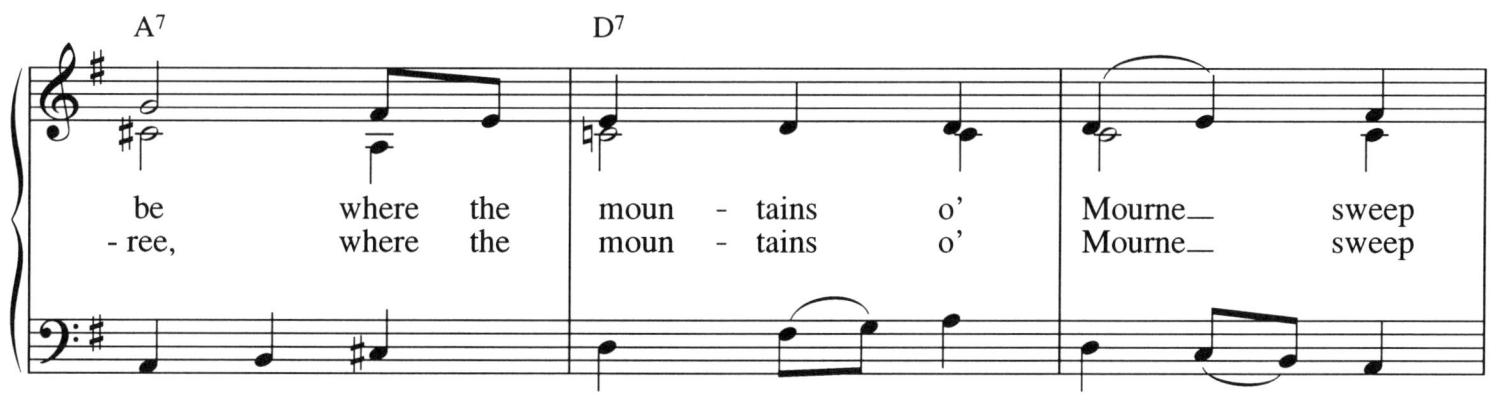

3. I've seen England's king from the top of a bus;
   I never knew him, tho' he means to know us.
   And, tho' by the Saxon we once were oppressed,
   Still I cheered (God forgive me!), I cheered with the rest.
   And, now that he's visited Erin's green shore,
   We'll be much better friends than we've been heretofore.
   When we've got all we want, we're as quiet as can be
   Where the mountains o' Mourne sweep down to the sea.

4. You remember young Peter O'Loughlin, of course?
   Well, now he is here at the head of the force.
   I met him today, I was crossin' the Strand,
   And he stopped the whole street wid wan wave of his hand.
   And there we stood talkin' of days that are gone,
   While the whole population of London looked on.
   But, for all these great powers, he's wishful, like me,
   To be back where dark Mourne sweeps down to the sea.

5. There's beautiful girls here - oh, nivver you mind! -
   Wid beautiful shapes nature niver designed,
   And lovely complexions, all roses and crame;
   But O'Loughlin remarked, wid regard to the same,
   That "If those roses you venture to sip,
   The colours might all come away on your lip."
   So I'll wait for the wild rose that's waitin' for me
   Where the mountains o' Mourne sweep down to the sea.

The Spinning Wheel

Words & Music by John Francis Waller & Delia Murphy

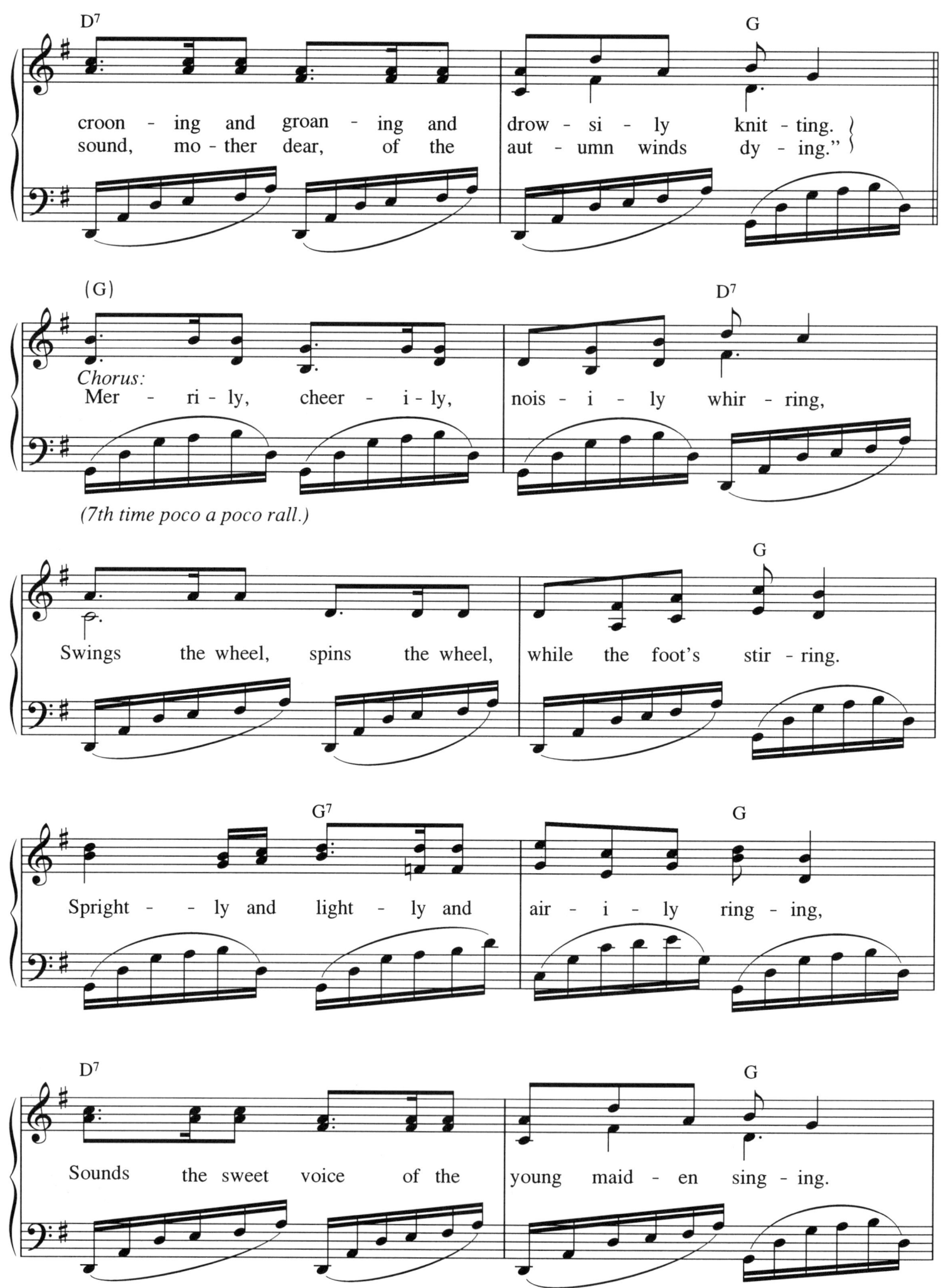

3. "What's that noise that I hear at the window, I wonder?"
   "'Tis the little birds chirping the holly-bush under."
   "What makes you be pushing and moving your stool on,
   And singing all wrong that old song of Coolin?"

4. There's a form at the casement, the form of her true love,
   And he whispers with face bent "I'm waiting for you, love.
   Get up on the stool, through the lattice step lightly,
   And we'll rove the grove while the moon's shining brightly."

5. The maid shakes her head, on her lips lays her fingers,
   Steals up from the seat, longs to go and yet lingers;
   A frightened glance turns to her drowsy grandmother,
   Puts one foot on the stool, spins the wheel with the other.

6. Lazily, easily, swings now the wheel round,
   Slowly and lowly is heard now the reel's sound.
   Noiseless and light, to the lattice above her
   The maid steps, then leaps to the arms of her lover.

7. Slower and slower and slower the wheel swings,
   Lower and lower and lower the reel rings.
   'Ere the reel and the wheel stop their spinning and moving,
   Through the grove the young lovers by moonlight are roving.

Too-Ra-Loo-Ra-Loo-Ral (That's An Irish Lullaby)
Words & Music by J. R. Shannon

When Irish Eyes Are Smiling

Words by George Graff & Chauncey Olcott
Music by Ernest Ball

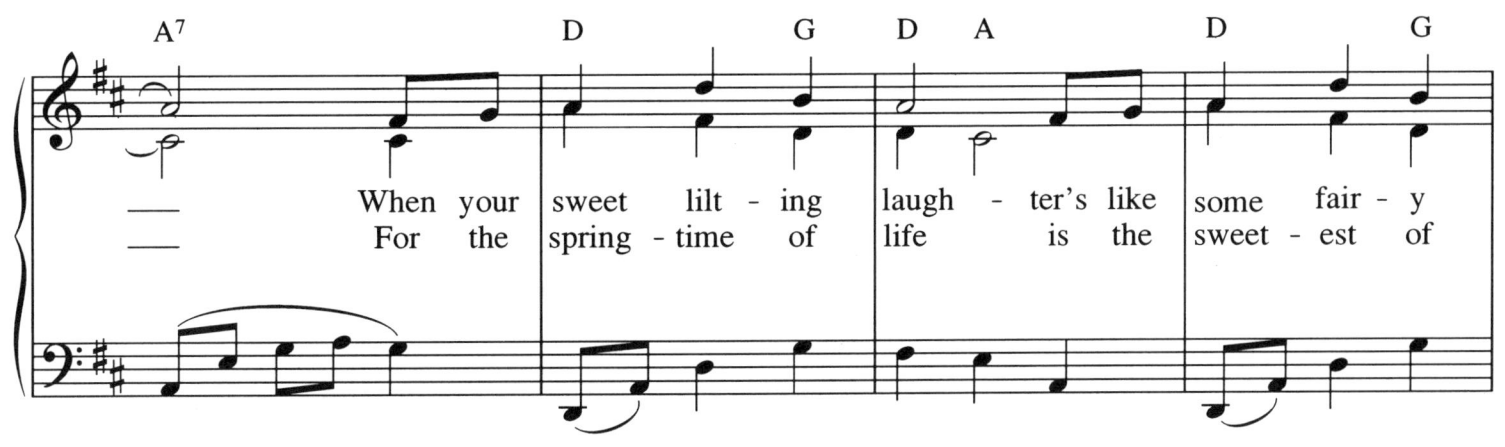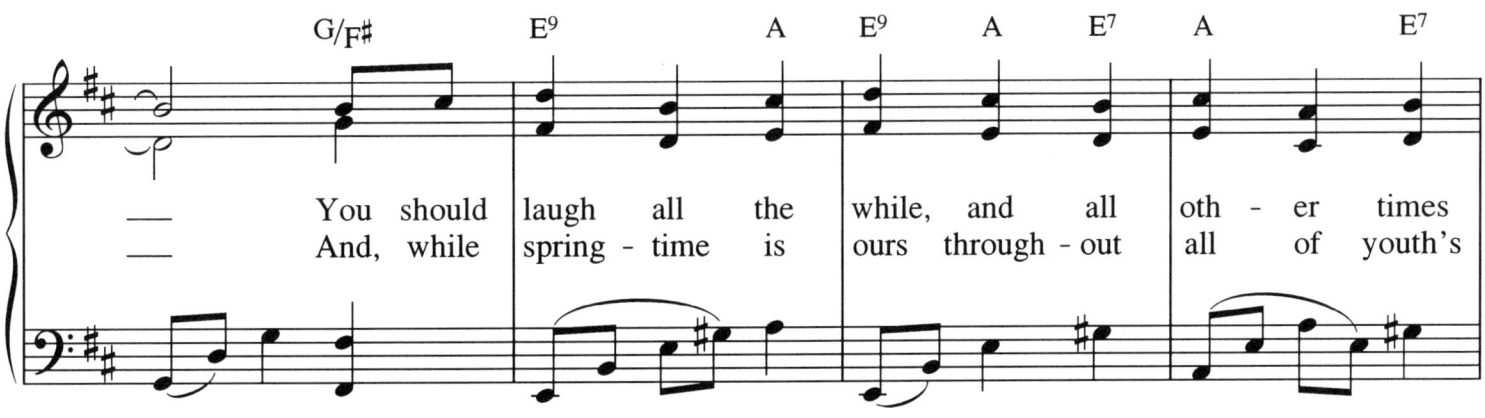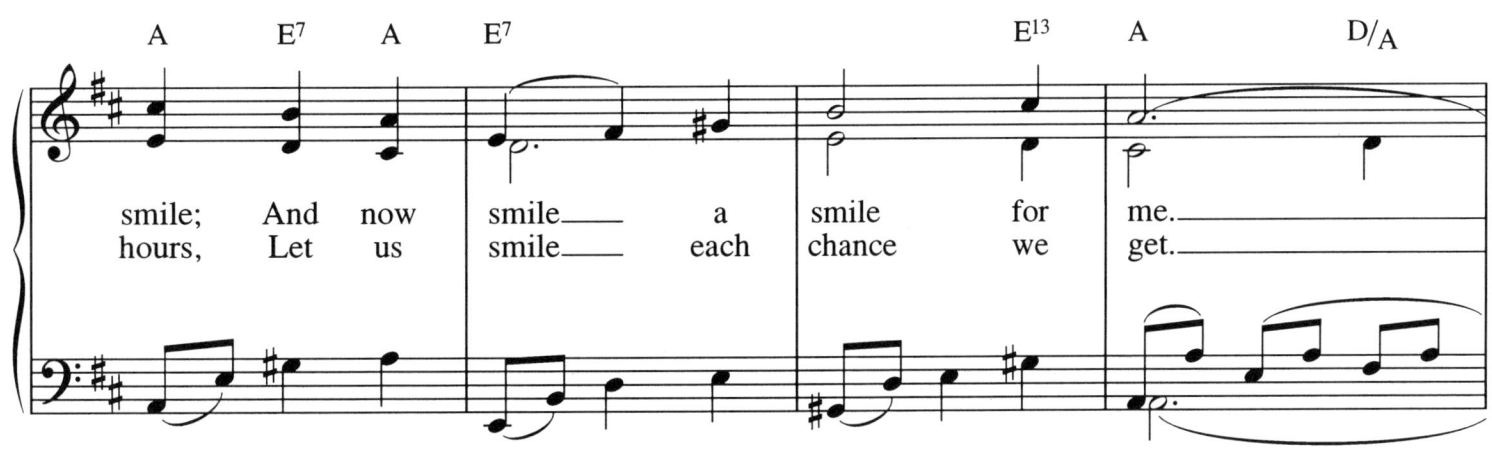

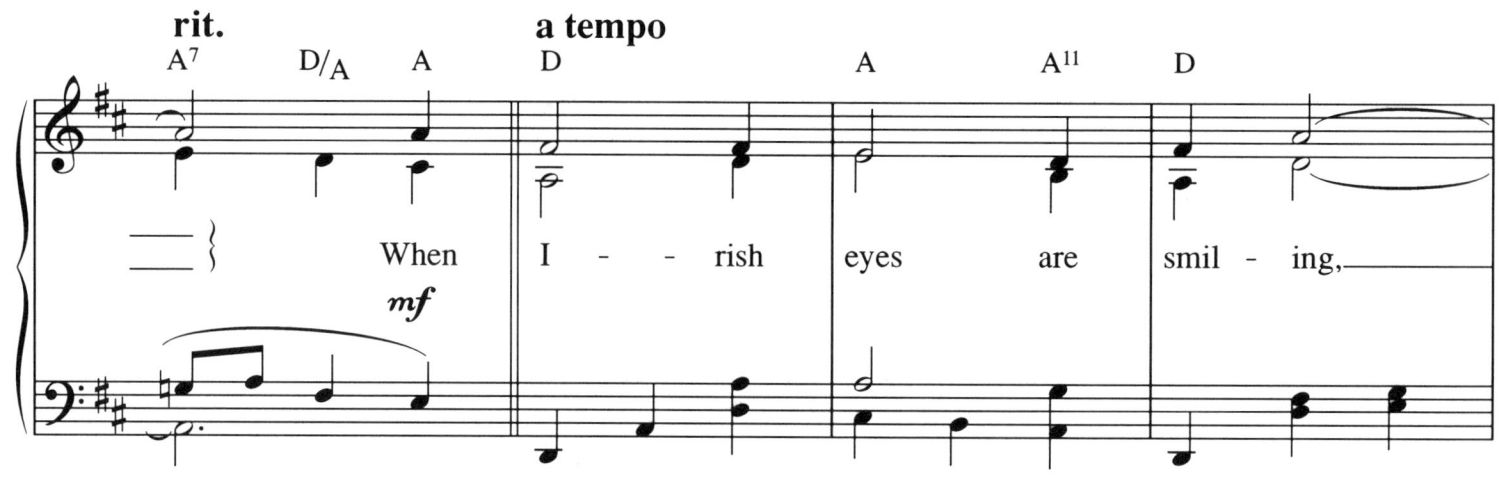
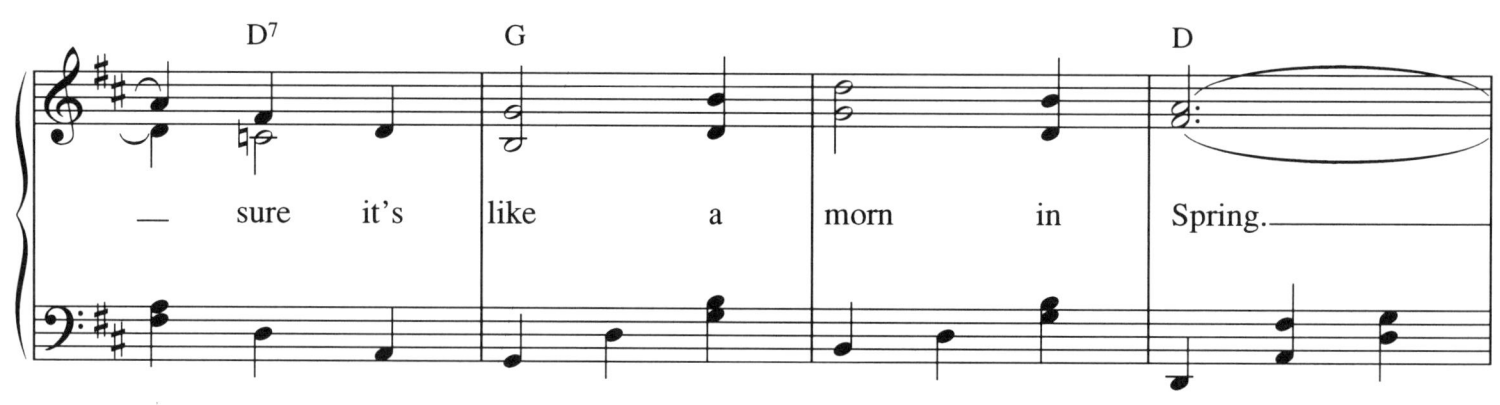

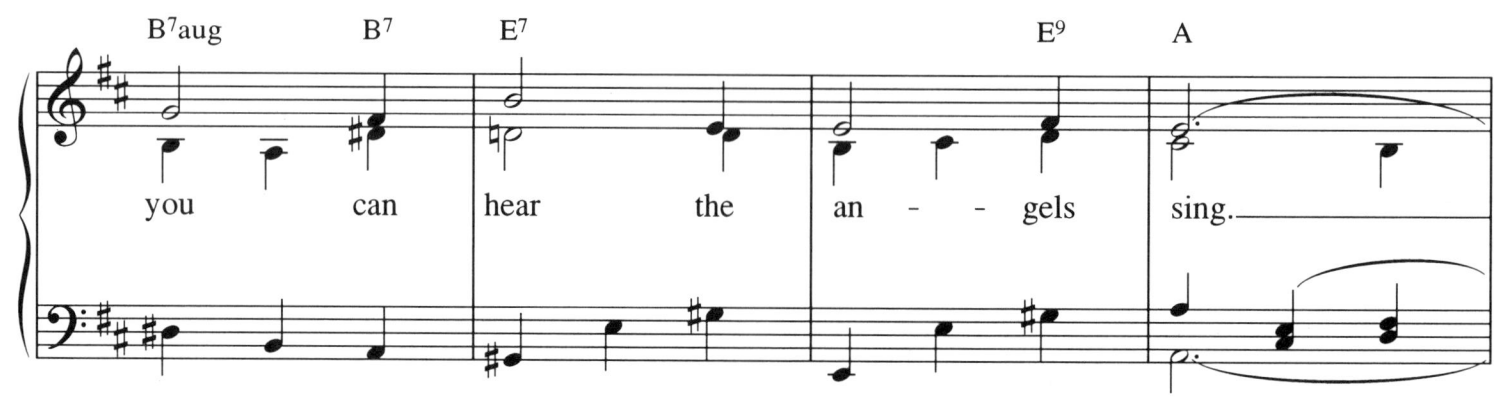

Whistling Gypsy (The Gypsy Rover)

Words & Music by Leo Maguire

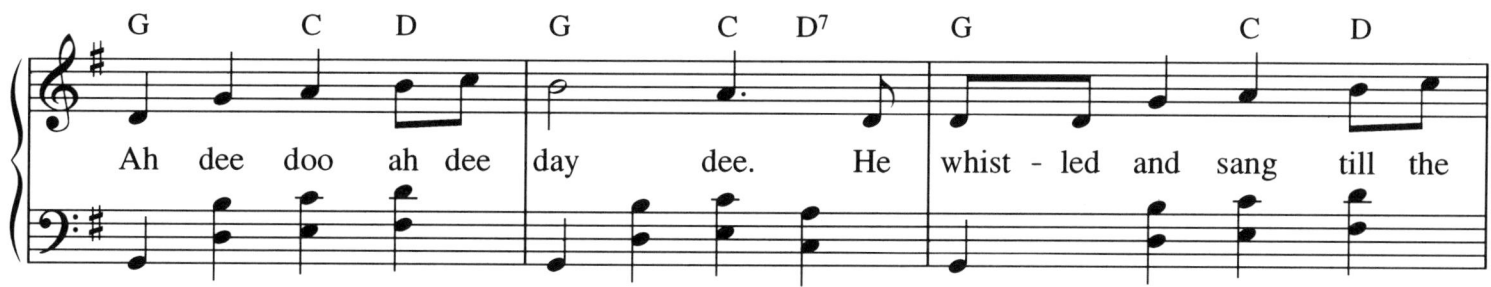
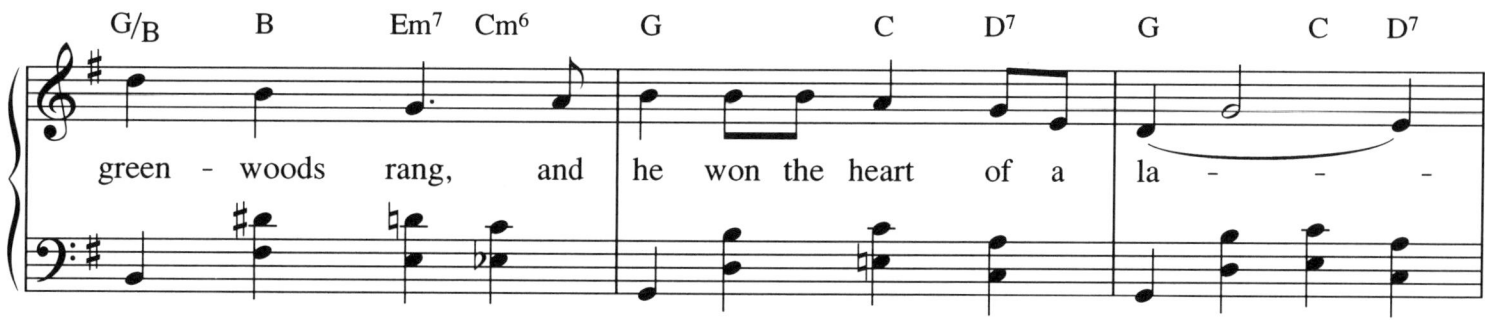

3. Her father saddled up his fastest steed,
   He ranged the valleys over;
   He sought his daughter at great speed,
   And the whistling gypsy rover.
   (Chorus)

4. He came at last to a mansion fine,
   Down by the River Clady;
   And there was music and there was wine
   For the gypsy and his lady.
   (Chorus)

5. "He is no gypsy, Father dear,
   But lord of all these lands all over.
   I'm going to stay till my dying day
   With the whistling gypsy rover!"
   (Chorus)